THOMAS CRANMER

THOMAS CRANMER

Colin Hamer

PUBLISHING WITH A MISSION

EP BOOKS
Faverdale North
Darlington, DL3 0PH, England

web: http://www.epbooks.org
e-mail: sales@epbooks.org

133 North Hanover Street
Carlisle, PA 17013, USA

www.epbooks.us
e-mail: usasales@epbooks.org

First published 2012

British Library Cataloguing in Publication Data available

ISBN 13: 978-0-85234-773-7   ISBN: 0-85234-773-1

Printed and bound in Great Britain by Martins the Printers Ltd, Berwick-upon-Tweed.

For Chris Hogg and her daughter Sarah,
whom, sadly, I never met

CONTENTS

Author's note

It is hoped that this small book will help to introduce a wider readership to Thomas Cranmer, a key figure of the English Reformation. He was, as James in the New Testament describes Elijah, 'a man subject to like passions as we are', but nonetheless a hero of the faith as so clearly and courageously demonstrated on the day of his martyrdom.

If this book had been a biography of John Calvin (1509–1564), Cranmer's more famous contemporary, I might have been overwhelmed by the task of digesting the material that has been written about him in the last fifty years alone. This is not the case with Thomas Cranmer. The modern literature on him is sparse, but is dominated by Diarmaid MacCulloch's magisterial account *Thomas Cranmer*, published in 1996. Although I have drawn on a wide variety of sources available on the Tudor period, it is Professor MacCulloch's book I found myself turning to most. Anybody wanting to explore further the life of Cranmer after reading this short biography could do no better than to start there. Furthermore, I would like to thank Day One Publications for giving me permission to reuse some of the material from my own biography of Anne Boleyn published by them in 2007.

To maintain narrative flow, explanations of any specific Christian doctrines (for example, on the Eucharist) have on the whole been omitted, but to avoid ambiguity a glossary has been provided.

PREFACE

Thomas Cranmer, one of the Reformation's most famous martyrs, can accurately be described as the architect of the Church of England and, consequently, of the worldwide Anglican communion. Despite this, compared with other key figures of the Reformation, little has been written about him in recent years.

This omission is both remarkable and understandable: remarkable, because undoubtedly Crammer's involvement in England's break with the historic Roman Church was crucial — a break which formed the foundation for the freedom of the gospel in England for the next 450 years; understandable, because his was no dramatic conversion loved by storytellers — rather, he undertook a lifetime journey away from the Roman sacramental system to an understanding that heaven was the gift of God to all those whom he loves. Furthermore, despite the fact that we are all fallen men and women, we so often want to see our heroes as giants, able to cope with every situation life throws at them without faltering — Cranmer was not such a man.

This book looks to assess his life from the perspective of a twenty-first-century evangelical Christian — that is, someone who accepts the Bible as the final authority on what God requires of men and women in this life. It is a term that Cranmer, as he neared his famous, dreadful and glorious end, would have been happy to have applied to himself.

INTRODUCTION

In 1525, England was a Roman Catholic nation, a faithful outpost of Rome. The pope had awarded King Henry VIII (1491–1547) the title 'Defender of the Faith' for upholding the church's doctrine of the Seven Sacraments against the teaching of Martin Luther (1483–1546). But by 1535, England had rejected the 'mother church', embraced the 'new learning' of the emerging evangelicals and had started on the road to being what many would term today a Protestant nation with an established church that owed no allegiance to Rome.

It is difficult for the twenty-first-century mind to envisage the dynamics of this on the contemporary religious and social situation of the time. Perhaps, if it could be imagined that in the next ten years England became an Islamic state with the current Archbishop of Canterbury presiding as its chief imam, the monarch having played a significant part in the transition, this might give us a flavour of the turbulent times that were the hallmark of sixteenth-century England. Yet all this was achieved without revolution or invasion. How had it happened?

Although there were many personalities and complex forces at play, four characters dominated. Henry VIII, married to the Spanish Catherine of Aragon (1485–1536), was the unpredictable, all-powerful king. But in 1522, a vivacious young woman, Anne Boleyn (1501–1536), a daughter of a courtier, arrived home from France in time to attend the Christmas celebrations at the Tudor court. Henry was soon besotted. Anne was highly intelligent: a linguist, musician and dancer — but more significantly, she had come to faith in Christ during her time abroad. It soon became clear to all that she was no ordinary debutante or potential plaything of the king; she was immensely principled and courageous, and prepared to make a stand for her newfound faith. That relationship, and Anne's eventual marriage to Henry in 1532, set England on the road to a totally new mindset and outlook as increasing numbers of people rejected the teachings of the Roman Church.

The power came from the throne, but the midwife of the transition was Thomas Cromwell (1485–1540), distant ancestor of the famous Oliver Cromwell, and a political genius who put his weight behind the new learning, although seemingly never embracing for himself the Saviour it spoke of. But still a key figure is missing. Where was the gifted theologian needed to effect this immense change in English national life? Our fourth character, the Cambridge University academic Thomas Cranmer, emerged on the scene as a result of a 'chance' meeting in 1529. Without him it is difficult to see that the road Henry VIII pushed the nation down would ever have been successfully navigated.

Cranmer was plucked from relative obscurity and thrust into the highest ecclesiastical office in the land, being appointed Archbishop of Canterbury in 1533. He was not a natural public figure; he could be timid, even frightened. At difficult times he would prevaricate, and when in a tight corner, he would often make a compromise. He would sometimes be confused and baffled by the turn of events, yet his impact on English national life in subsequent centuries has been immense.

Furthermore, he was prepared, at the end, to make the supreme sacrifice for his faith. On the last day of his earthly life, Thomas Cranmer, who like his famous New Testament namesake, had prevaricated and doubted, doubted and prevaricated no more and openly declared for his Saviour and the gospel. The man who had so often not wanted to 'rock the boat' stunned Christendom with a display of moral and physical courage rarely paralleled in the history of mankind.

TIMELINE

10 November 1483	Martin Luther born
2 July 1489	Thomas Cranmer born
14 November 1501	Catherine of Aragon marries Arthur, Henry VII's eldest son
1503	Cranmer goes to Cambridge University
12 April 1509	Henry VIII crowned
11 June 1509	Henry VIII marries Catherine of Aragon
7 July 1509	John Calvin born
1514	Cranmer becomes a Fellow of Jesus College, Cambridge
18 February 1516	Catherine gives birth to Mary — eventually Mary I
31 October 1517	Martin Luther presents his 95 objections to Catholic teaching and practice
11 October 1521	Henry VIII declared defender of the Catholic faith by the pope

1526	Cranmer becomes Doctor of Divinity at Cambridge
1526	The great 'divorce' debate starts
June 1527	Henry tells Catherine he wants an annulment of their marriage
1529	Cranmer comes to the king's attention
1531	Henry VIII officially separates from Catherine of Aragon
1532	Cranmer marries Margaret
14 November 1532	Anne Boleyn marries Henry at a secret ceremony in Dover
30 March 1533	Cranmer is appointed Archbishop of Canterbury
23 May 1533	Cranmer annuls Catherine's marriage to Henry VIII
7 September 1533	Anne Boleyn gives birth to Elizabeth — to become Elizabeth I
19 September 1535	The evangelicals Foxe, Latimer and Hilsey consecrated as bishops
1535	Thomas Cromwell appointed vicegerent
7 January 1536	Catherine of Aragon dies
19 May 1536	Anne Boleyn is executed
30 May 1536	Henry VIII marries Jane Seymour
6 October 1536	William Tyndale is martyred
12 October 1537	Edward VI born
24 October 1537	Jane Seymour dies
1539	Cranmer's (The Great) Bible is printed
6 January 1540	Henry VIII marries Anne of Cleves
9 July 1540	Cranmer annuls Henry VIII's marriage to Anne of Cleves
28 July 1540	Henry VIII marries Catherine Howard

28 July 1540	Thomas Cromwell is executed
13 February 1542	Catherine Howard is executed
12 July 1543	Henry VIII marries Catherine Parr
September 1543	Cranmer investigates his own heresy
28 January 1547	Henry VIII dies, succeeded by Edward VI
9 June 1549	The new *Prayer Book* introduced
July 1551	The Stranger Church set up
April 1552	A further version of the *Prayer Book* is authorized
9 June 1553	The *42 Articles* issued
6 July 1553	Edward VI dies
July 1553	Cranmer involved in Lady Jane Grey's claim to the throne
20 August 20 1553	Mary I declared queen
14 September 1553	Cranmer arrested and sent to the Tower
13 November 1553	Cranmer tried for treason and condemned to death
12 September 1555	Cranmer tried for heresy
28 January 1556	Cranmer signs his first recantation
18 March 1556	Cranmer signs his last recantation
21 March 1556	Cranmer is burnt at the stake
17 November 1558	Mary I dies; Elizabeth I (Anne Boleyn's daughter) becomes queen
24 March 1603	Elizabeth I dies and the Tudor dynasty ends

1

THE EARLY YEARS

Sixteenth-century England

Any assessment of a life has to take into account the time when it was lived. But as we move into the twenty-first century, it becomes increasingly difficult to understand a life lived in sixteenth-century Europe. Today the West has largely replaced theistic religion with the theory of evolution to explain our origins, and, in turn, it has embraced pluralism, diversity, moral relativism, and seen a rapid pace of change both in technology and ideas. The concept of a Judgement Day when all will stand before their Creator has, on the whole, been rejected. There is for most a clear separation of Church and state, the secular and religious, and religion in turn is seen to be essentially a private matter.

But Europe in the fifteenth and sixteenth centuries was only just emerging from a medieval Catholicism where there was one truth, one heaven, one hell, one great Judgement Day to come, and all authority lay with the pope in Rome who presided over a church which decided where your eternal destiny lay. Church and state were one, and most people still thought that the Earth itself was fixed in the centre of the heavens, with the sun and stars rotating round it. Most of the scientific advances which we take for granted lay afar off in the future; a life lived in 1500 was very much like a life lived in any previous century.

For more than a thousand years Christendom had believed what the Roman Catholic Church had taught — that Christ's work on the cross and all the favours of heaven belonged to the church; only the church could administer the benefits of heaven through its own sacramental system. These sacraments, it taught, were the means by which man received God's favour or 'grace', without which you were destined for hell. Kings and queens, rich and poor, all had to come to the church. Heaven was entered only through its gates; truly it had the keys to heaven and hell. And the issue went deeper. It did not affect only matters 'spiritual': the church also believed that all earthly powers were ultimately subject to its authority.

For anybody to arrive safely in heaven a constant supply of grace was required, received principally by a continuous observance of the church's rituals but also dispensed at shrines. These often housed at least one 'relic' — items that are believed to have come from a saint, one of the original apostles, or even Christ himself. They were all thought to have a sort of 'magic' property, so to touch or even to see such an item might 'confer grace'. The church taught then (as it does today) that when the bread and wine are consecrated by the priest in the church service known as the Mass, they actually become the body and blood of Christ — the supreme 'relic' that confers grace. When a Mass was performed on behalf of a deceased loved one it was thought to speed their journey through purgatory and on towards heaven.

It was against this background that Martin Luther burst onto the scene and challenged virtually everything that the church had taught. This new learning quickly spread across the Continent and into England with profound effect on many. Some, as we shall see, like Cranmer, embraced the good news of the gospel brought out into the open after being hidden for so long; others, like Thomas Cromwell, saw the new world order ushered in by the theological revolution as an opportunity for personal advancement and wealth.

Birth and early education

Thomas Cranmer was born in fairly humble circumstances in 1489 in Aslockton, Nottinghamshire, England. His family had arrived in the village from Lincolnshire in the early 1400s when his great-grandfather had married the daughter of a well-placed (but not wealthy) local family. Not deemed large enough for a parish church, Aslockton had a small chapel — now with a plaque describing itself as 'Cranmer's Cottage'.

Thomas' elder brother John received the principal share of the inheritance on his father's death in 1501, while Thomas and his other brother Edmond received a small annual allowance to ensure their education in preparation for a career in the church. There were at least two sisters, one of which became a Cistercian nun. It is probable that Thomas started his education in the local village school where he was taught by a 'rude parish clerk' before going off to grammar school where he suffered at the hands of a 'marvellous severe and cruel schoolmaster'. It was not for

long, because at the age of fourteen he went up to the newly
founded Jesus College at Cambridge. It was a lengthy eight
years before he became a Bachelor of Arts in 1511, although
he became a Master of Arts just three years later. Cranmer
readily admitted to being a slow reader, always with pencil in
hand ready to diligently mark anything that interested him.
His contemporaries at Cambridge included Hugh Latimer
(1487–1555), who was martyred in 1555; and the famous
Roman Catholic and humanist, Erasmus (1466–1536), who
was invited to teach there from 1511. It is certain that he
would have been known to Cranmer.

Although a layman (not a priest or deacon in the church)
Cranmer was elected a fellow of his college in 1514, a
fellowship he had to give up when he married a local woman,
Joan, sometime in his late twenties. It seems that, after the
marriage, Thomas and Joan lodged separately, Joan staying
at a Dolphin Inn in Cambridge. This caused detractors later
in his life to claim that Joan was a 'low born' innkeeper's
daughter and that the marriage was forced on Cranmer
because of Joan's pregnancy. There is no evidence for either,
although undoubtedly the marriage had caused Cranmer to
sacrifice his employment and comfortable living quarters.
But soon, perhaps within a year, he lost both his wife and
their first child in childbirth. He was promptly offered his
old fellowship back, an indication of the regard Jesus College
had for him.

A Doctor of Divinity

By 1520, Cranmer had taken holy orders, becoming a
secular (that is, not church-based) priest, and in 1526,

having principally studied Scripture, he became a Doctor of Divinity and soon accepted a lectureship in the Old and New Testaments. It was at this time that Luther was generating controversy with his famous *Ninety-Five Theses* (nailed to the door of the castle church in Wittenberg), but relatively little is known about Cranmer's position on these matters during his three decades at Cambridge. He was certainly a careful and conscientious scholar who showed a high regard for Scripture and was fully aware of Luther's published work, but there is no clear evidence that he had any sympathy with Luther's cause, in fact rather the opposite. Bishop John Fisher (1469–1535) attacked Luther's teaching in a publication of 1523 and Cranmer made extensive marginal notes in his own copy on two separate occasions; the earlier set, seemingly dating between 1523 and 1532, joined with Fisher in consistently rebutting Luther's rejection of papal authority. This was at a time when nascent Reformers such as William Tyndale (1494–1536), Hugh Latimer (*c.* 1487–1555) and Thomas Bilney (1495–1531) were meeting in the White Horse Inn in Cambridge, and rapidly coming to the conclusion that Scripture was the supreme authority in matters affecting man's final destiny. In light of this, it seems unlikely that Cranmer was one of their number, despite the claims of some biographers. But he was certainly giving consideration to the new learning coming from the Continent, and it is clear from some of the early notes he made in Fisher's book that he saw validity in some of Luther's points; signs of an independence of mind that would take a lifetime to fully flower.

Nonetheless, at this time Cranmer was considered fully orthodox and was selected by Cardinal Wolsey (1473–1530) to go on a minor diplomatic mission to Spain, after which

Cranmer vividly described the storms they experienced on his return journey in the Bay of Biscay and the emergency bailing out of the ship. Arriving at port in June 1527, he was taken by fast stagecoach to London for his first audience with Henry VIII. Within a few short years Cranmer would leave Cambridge University to embark on a journey that would prove far more turbulent than his voyage through the Bay of Biscay.

2

FROM ACADEMIC TO
ARCHBISHOP

The king's divorce

In our contemporary age of high-profile divorces, there is none to compare with the divorce which Henry VIII was trying to engineer from his wife Catherine of Aragon.[1] It was a divorce that not only separated Henry from his wife, it also split England from the historic Catholic Church and drove a wedge between England and mainland Europe. The resultant scar has never fully healed.

Catherine had previously been married to Henry's elder brother Arthur; he had been fifteen and she, within five months, was a widow at the age of sixteen, Arthur having died, probably of tuberculosis. The following year the twelve-year-old Henry had been officially betrothed to Catherine (Henry's father being keen to keep both the potential alliance with Spain alive and Catherine's substantial dowry in his coffers) — despite the fact that the young Henry was said to have expressed doubts about the validity of such a marriage the year before. These doubts were based on the Old Testament affinity laws, doubts that the then Archbishop of Canterbury, William Warham, and much of the rest of the church hierarchy shared.

The objections to the marriage were founded on two Bible verses: Leviticus 18:16 ('You shall not uncover the nakedness of your brother's wife; it is your brother's nakedness') and Leviticus 20:21 ('If a man takes his brother's wife, it is impurity. He has uncovered his brother's nakedness; they shall be childless'). The dilemma was that Deuteronomy seemed to contradict the teaching of Leviticus. Deuteronomy 25:5 says, 'If brothers dwell together, and one of them dies and has no son, the wife of the dead man shall not be married outside the family to a stranger. Her husband's brother shall go in to her and take her as his wife and perform the duty of a husband's brother to her.' Henry considered, along with others, that Deuteronomy belonged to the ceremonial law, which applied only to Jews, not to Christians, so Leviticus stood without qualification. But the Roman Church's position was that Deuteronomy and Leviticus both applied to Christians. Leviticus was outlining the general principle and Deuteronomy was giving a single exception — when the widow of your brother was childless. Henry's case fitted this exception precisely, but nonetheless it was decided that a papal dispensation was required, and it was duly received in April 1506. The marriage went ahead, but not until after Henry VII's death and Henry VIII's accession to the throne in 1509.

The correct explanation for the apparent contradiction within the biblical text is most likely that Leviticus 18:16 and 20:21 are referring to a living divorced brother. It is clear you cannot marry your brother's wife while they are still married, so the verse is saying you cannot marry your brother's wife even if they have divorced. He would be dishonoured on seeing his ex-wife with his own brother. Consequently, it is legitimate to marry the widow of your brother whether she is childless or not; there is therefore no contradiction with the teaching of Deuteronomy.

But by 1522, after thirteen years of marriage, Henry still had no male heir. Was the marriage blighted because it was against Scripture? The threat of childlessness in Leviticus 20 is probably referring to a legal position rather than actual childlessness. Deuteronomy 23:2 says, 'No one born of a forbidden union may enter the assembly of the LORD. Even to the tenth generation, none of his descendants may enter the assembly of the LORD.' In other words, there would be no legitimate heir to the family if the marriage was illegitimate (for example, if you had married your brother's wife while he was alive); the children would not be considered Jewish. It is unlikely, however, that this was Henry's perspective, and it is possible that his earlier doubts were now resurfacing. Furthermore, the lack of a male heir for the Tudor throne was a major concern. Princess Mary, aged eleven, was Henry VIII's only surviving legitimate child — Catherine had had one stillbirth, at least one miscarriage, and one child had survived just fifty-two days. She was approaching forty years old, and it is probable that Henry had been told that her child-bearing years were over. In theory there was nothing to stop a female succession, but it had never happened. Even if the throne successfully passed to Mary, any subsequent marriage of hers to a member of a foreign dynasty could see the throne and the kingdom pass to foreign hands.

Anne Boleyn

However, many think that the true motivation for Henry VIII's divorce was that, in 1522, there had been a new arrival at Henry's court: the charismatic and sophisticated Anne Boleyn. Fresh from the French court, Anne was familiar with Reformed literature and the new learning, as the evangelical teaching emanating from the Continent was called. Her fluency in French gave her the privileged position of reading the Bible for herself, and all the evidence points to the fact that she had come to a personal faith in the Saviour spoken of there. Furthermore, she possessed a copy of William Tyndale's *The Obedience of the Christian Man and How all Christian Rulers Ought to Govern*. She had marked passages of special interest and had shown them to Henry, despite the fact that it had been deemed heretical and banned from court by England's own Cardinal Wolsey. Tyndale's thesis was that all men should obey God's law, and that the concept of a separate authority for the pope and clergy was against the teaching of the Bible. Further, and one can imagine that this was particularly appealing to Henry, Tyndale believed that all men were subject to the earthly authority of the king, and that, in turn, the king was not subject to the separate authority of the Roman Catholic Church.

Henry's true motivation for the divorce will probably never be known, but it seems that the two things, the lack of a male heir and his desire for Anne Boleyn, coalesced in his mind and became a driving force for radical change. In 1529, the pope's representative (the papal legate), Campeggio, had arrived to adjudicate in the matter along with Cardinal Wolsey. Wolsey was backing the king (he realized his own future was closely tied to the outcome), but Catherine had appealed directly to the pope; thus, probably to Campeggio's relief, but certainly to Wolsey's distress, the matter was stalled.

A chance meeting with Cranmer

In that summer Cranmer, to escape an outbreak of the plague in Cambridge, went to stay with the Cressy family in Essex whose two sons he was tutoring. This family home was also the lodging place of Stephen Gardiner (d.1555) and Edward Foxe as they accompanied the king on the court's summer 'progress' — when a number of men from court would travel with the king within a hundred-mile radius of London, looking for the best hunting while staying at smaller Crown properties or with aristocratic friends.

Over dinner with the visitors, Cranmer suggested that Henry should give up on Rome and instead canvas the universities on their opinion of the divorce matter. It is reported that he said,

> If the King rightly understood his own office, neither Pope, nor any other potentate whatsoever, neither in causes civil nor ecclesiastical, hath anything to do with him or any of his actions, within his own realm and dominion; but he himself, under God, hath the supreme government of this land in all causes whatsoever.

It was not an especially new or radical idea, and Cranmer was somewhat surprised to be subsequently summoned to his second meeting with Henry, who asked him to write his thoughts in the form of a treatise at the home of Thomas

Boleyn, Anne Boleyn's father. Thomas Boleyn, despite the way he is portrayed in some twenty-first-century media, was the most able French speaker at Henry's court, a favourite jousting partner of Henry's, and was described by Erasmus as 'extremely learned'. There is no evidence that Cranmer knew the Boleyn family before this time, but it is certain that he now formed a warm attachment to them.

Cranmer was now a trusted royal advisor, one that MacCulloch claims demonstrated 'clear cool analysis', and that 'All through his life, Cranmer was either blessed or cursed with the ability to see his opponents' point of view: an attribute rare enough in any age, but in particularly short supply during the Reformation.'

Cranmer travels on the Continent

Cranmer was subsequently sent with Thomas Boleyn on a diplomatic mission to meet the Holy Roman Emperor and the pope. Much of his time there was spent gathering opinions from the universities, and on his return to England, Cranmer continued to work on the annulment. The issue at stake was papal authority: Did canon law (that is, church law covering such things as the church's own government and organization) give the pope authority to grant the original dispensation for Henry's marriage with Catherine? It was in December 1529 that Parliament, at the king's direction, had accepted the reinstatement of the charge of 'praemunire', whereby individuals could be convicted of a crime and fined for appealing to any power outside of the realm (for example, the pope), for resolution of a situation within England. The king duly accused the English clergy of the same, specifically for having accepted Cardinal Wolsey as the pope's representative, even though that had been at Henry's own insistence. The clergy reluctantly, but probably wisely, paid up.

When on the Continent with Thomas Boleyn, Cranmer had had contact with the continental Reformers, including Martin Bucer (1491–1551), but he and others, for example Luther and Philipp Melanchthon (1497–1560), and indeed England's own William Tyndale, had little sympathy for Henry's proposed divorce. And although Cranmer was now beginning to doubt papal authority, he still would not have been thought of as an evangelical who, like Luther, stood on Scripture alone; there was still a considerable gap between their different theological outlooks. At Cranmer's trial in 1555, the judge said of Cranmer, referring to this time of his life,

> *Who was thought of as then more devout? ... who was thought to have more conscience of a vow-making, and observing the order of the church, more earnest in the defence of the real presence of Christ's body and blood in the sacrament of the altar, than ye were?*

Cranmer marries

In 1532, Cranmer was on the Continent again, and at Nuremberg he saw the practical outworking of the Reformation instigated by Luther. It was during the summer of this visit that Cranmer married again, this time a niece of Andreas Osiander (1498–1552), one of the Reformation's notable theologians. Some historians see that in this Cranmer was violating a vow of celibacy, but others claim that such had been dropped from the English Church's ordination process some years previously.

It was while on the Continent that Cranmer saw the death and destruction that had been wrought in Austria by Italian troops who had come into the country to rescue it from Turkish hordes. There was talk of insurrection, and Cranmer had written to Henry VIII about his fear of any popular revolt. It is perhaps this same fear that was responsible for his cautious approach to church reforms in later life, an approach that annoyed his more zealous colleagues.

Meanwhile, back in England, Archbishop Warham had died, and Henry had decided, to the surprise of most, not least Cranmer, that Cranmer should be the successor. A letter was duly despatched to the archbishop designate on 1 October ordering him to return and to take up his appointment. The newly married, reluctant and bewildered Cranmer took his time on the homeward journey, undoubtedly wondering what life had in store for him now.

Henry marries Anne Boleyn

Back in England, Cranmer's elevation was undoubtedly seen as a triumph for the Boleyn family and as a reward for his work on the annulment, the most pressing issue on his return in January 1533. However, it is thought that by this time Henry had already taken the initiative and married Anne Boleyn in a secret ceremony in Dover on 14 November 1532. On 25 January 1533, a more formal wedding ceremony was conducted, but still in private. The ceremony probably took place before dawn over the Holbein Gate of Whitehall. The priest asked if Henry had the pope's permission; Henry replied that he had a document giving him licence to marry. Henry did indeed have a licence from the pope to marry Anne Boleyn, but it was conditional upon the declaration that his marriage to Catherine was void. It did not specify who would make that declaration, and Henry was relying on Cranmer for just that. But the appointment of the new archbishop had to wait, ironically, for the papal paperwork — the 'bulls' of appointment.

Cranmer appointed archbishop

Once these arrived in late March events moved apace. On 14 March Thomas Cromwell presented a bill before Parliament, 'The Act of Appeals', which would put on the statute book a statement of royal supremacy and would forbid appeals to the pope on religious matters; they were instead to be settled by the English monarch — the break with Rome was made. On 26 March Convocation (the church's parliament) under Cranmer's presidency decided (although there was much vocal opposition) that the pope had not had the authority to issue a dispensation for Henry's marriage to Catherine. Cranmer was duly consecrated on 30 March, but he had objected to swearing any oath of loyalty to the pope, and a revised wording had had to be hurriedly accepted by the Privy Council. Cranmer had further made it clear that, in giving the revised oath, he did not intend to bind himself to anything that went against the law of God or the prerogatives of the king. Cranmer here was not articulating a new idea, the previous year the Privy Council had expressed its own dislike of any oath of allegiance to the pope, and the following year it was abolished by statute.

After all the debate and prevarication of the previous years, the relevant procedures to finally resolve the divorce issue had been pushed through Convocation and Parliament within a matter of days. Henry's marriage was declared null, and Catherine was told to change her title to that of dowager Princess of Wales. In Cranmer's defence, it might be pointed out that none of these steps were initiated by him; his part was to pronounce whether he thought the decision of Pope Julius II in granting a dispensation for the first marriage was lawful or not, and he had decided it was not. Nonetheless, Cranmer, the careful academic, had in these bold and, many would say, reckless moves become the key facilitator of the annulment of Henry's marriage and England's break with Rome. On Easter Sunday 1533 Anne went to Mass as Henry's wife and the *de facto* queen.

To silence dissenters within the church sympathetic to Catherine, Cranmer forbade any clerical preaching unless it was authorized by him. As was noted at the time, the irony that Cranmer should 'forbid that the word of God should be preached in the church throughout his diocese' was not lost. Furthermore, Cranmer had accepted his appointment from the pope while at the same rejecting papal authority, and he had become the chief cleric of a church that taught clerical celibacy while remaining married to Margaret, a marriage he kept secret from virtually all his contemporaries and certainly from Henry. The reader will have to make their own judgement about Cranmer's personal ethics in these decisions and whether the turbulent and dangerous times justified his actions. It is a recurring problem in any assessment of Cranmer's life, and it will be addressed again in the final chapter.

In any event our Cambridge don was now the Primate of the church in England, close to the king, and a member of a select group of advisors that formed the Privy Council; in effect a senior churchman and politician who would play a lead role in the Reformation in England. Many would see that he was singularly unsuited to either of the newly acquired roles that destiny had thrust upon him.

Anne crowned queen

However, the die had been cast and Anne's coronation day was set for Sunday 1 June 1533. On Thursday 29 May, Anne was brought by water from Greenwich to the Tower of London. There was much pageantry, both on the streets of London and on the river, where many large barges had been prepared with covered cabins. Finally came Anne herself, bareheaded as tradition dictated, her unfashionably dark hair on display for all to see, a fact commented upon by Cranmer. Special stands had been erected in the Abbey, including one for the king where he could watch proceedings hidden behind a latticework screen — it was Anne's day. Mass was said and at the climax of events Anne Boleyn was anointed and then crowned queen by Cranmer.

Confusing times

1533 had brought Cranmer a meteoric rise to power, but where did he stand theologically at this point? He had clearly shown (at least to himself) that he was against clerical celibacy. Furthermore he was in friendly correspondence with Erasmus who, although more of a humanist than a Reformer, certainly took the side of the Reformers on many issues. But the confusing nature of these times is no more clearly displayed than in Cranmer's adjudication of John Frith (1503–1533), one of his first tasks as archbishop. Frith, a Cambridge graduate and known associate of prominent evangelicals, had been with Tyndale in Antwerp but was arrested on his return in 1532 for his denial of the real presence in the Eucharist service. In the Tower, rather than maintaining a low profile and so keeping any hope for an acquittal alive, he wrote prolifically against the teaching of the church that Christ was actually present in the bread and wine when consecrated by the priest during the Mass. Frith was not saying anything different to Luther, but nonetheless he was consigned to the flames.

Could Cranmer have done more to save Frith? Certainly at this early stage Cranmer was displaying evangelical credentials, defending Hugh Latimer who, as Bishop of Worcester, was creating trouble with his forthright preaching from Scripture. It was Cranmer himself who had urged Latimer to preach 'according to the pure sense and meaning' of the text. He gave instruction to the Worcester Cathedral Priory that monks should attend Scripture readings for an hour a day and that this was to take precedence over other rituals; and what is more, that the Scripture should be expounded in English 'according to at least the literal sense'. This was at a time when, if Scripture was preached on at all, its plain meaning was eschewed in favour of highly allegorical (some might say bizarre) interpretations. Cranmer himself that summer of 1533 pursued an energetic programme in London, Leicester, Worcester and Croydon, of what was thought of at the time as evangelical preaching.

So why didn't Cranmer make a stand for John Frith? Was this a display of confused thinking, or worse, a weak character? But at this stage, Cranmer accepted the Roman Catholic belief in the real presence of Christ in the Mass; and he had not brought Frith to trial, it was a situation that he had inherited. His failure to reach out to Frith with whom he shared many beliefs is as much about our difficulty in understanding the nature of the times as it is about any lack of moral courage by Cranmer.

The Frith affair demonstrates that Cranmer's evangelical beliefs were still at a nascent stage, but from now on he had a powerful ally. Anne's influence on the religious map of England before she came to the throne was considerable; as queen she became a powerful driving force of the Reformation in England. Throughout her short time on the throne she pressed for and nominated for clerical appointments men who were known for their evangelical views. She remained a close friend and loyal supporter of Cranmer, and he in turn undoubtedly acted as a pastor to her. MacCulloch comments that Anne's reign would 'permanently shape Cranmer's life'.

Note

1. To be technically accurate, it was an annulment that Henry sought. The Church of Rome, then and now, does not recognize divorce but can find grounds to annul a marriage if its validity is open to doubt.

3

THE EARLY YEARS
WITH HENRY VIII

Cromwell as vicegerent

In 1535, Henry appointed Thomas Cromwell to the newly created post of 'vicegerent' which in effect gave Cromwell control of the king's newly separated church and eclipsed Thomas Cranmer as its principal minister. Was this because Henry realized his new archbishop was not ideally suited to the many demands of the new role that had been thrust upon him? Demands that Henry thought the Machiavellian political genius Thomas Cromwell was more able to fill? More likely it was to give Henry a lever of power over the nascent church, newly cast adrift from the papacy in Rome. The relationship between the vicegerent and the Archbishop of Canterbury was that of wise statesman advising the newly appointed evangelical archbishop; but inevitably, in light of Cromwell's skills and thirst for power and influence, it meant that Cranmer became the junior partner. It is certain that it was Cromwell, not Cranmer, who saw through the dissolution of the monasteries, one of the most high profile casualties of the Reformation in England. There is no evidence that Cranmer resented the appointment, even though he lost some of his own lands in the dissolution process; rather the reverse, as it meant that he was free to pursue what interested him, the cause of the gospel as he understood it at that stage.

1535 also brought the execution of Thomas More (1478–1535) and John Fisher. They had famously held out against Henry's marriage to Anne Boleyn, resisted the break with Rome, and then refused to swear the Oath of Succession that removed Mary's claim to the throne. Although Cranmer was present in 1535 at the final interrogation of More, there is no record of any contribution from him; it was Chancellor Audley and Cromwell who took the lead. Cranmer later claimed that he was against More's execution, and there is no reason to doubt him. He had written to Cromwell begging that they (More and Fisher) should be allowed to swear the Oath of Succession after their own fashion.

In the same year, there was another man whom Cranmer could not save, though he certainly wanted to. This was the fugitive Bible translator William Tyndale, now held in prison in Brussels. But even Cromwell's intervention did not avail. He was tried, strangled to death while his body was tied to the stake, and burned.

Anne Boleyn's downfall

Then in 1536 came Anne Boleyn's downfall. Thomas Cromwell played a key part in this and, despite much speculation, it is not entirely clear why. One possible reason was that Anne was never happy about the dissolution of the monasteries; she wanted them reformed and used as a basis for evangelical teaching. Anne saw that if they were broken up and the lands sold, the only beneficiaries would be Henry's friends and those he wanted to influence; nothing would be gained for the evangelical cause. When the dissolution of the monasteries bill was passed, it contained a personal veto for the king; in other words, Henry could reprieve any monastery he so chose. Cromwell knew that he would have to battle against Anne's influence with Henry if she appealed to the king to make a special case for any monastery she considered worth saving. Cromwell now realized that he was caught between Henry and Anne. Henry was keen on pushing through the dissolution to get the income into the exchequer, Anne was not. If Cromwell agreed with Anne that some should be saved, he antagonized the king; if he supported Henry's aggressive secularization, he antagonized Anne. Before she was queen, Anne had challenged Henry about Cardinal Wolsey's loyalty; Wolsey (Cromwell's former employer) had been summoned to appear before Henry but died before he had to face the consequences. Cromwell was acutely aware of Anne's hold over Henry.

Furthermore, Cromwell had secretly started talks with Charles V, the Holy Roman Emperor. Cromwell wanted to see the relationship between the empire and England restored after the turbulence caused by the break from the papacy. But Charles V wanted, as part of the arrangement, Mary's claim to the throne legitimized (a fact unknown to Henry). Not only was Mary Charles V's cousin, but the emperor saw that if Mary eventually succeeded to the throne it would cement the relationship with England. Cromwell did not see a problem in all of this, but it was a serious misreading of the situation. When Henry found out, he was furious; he would not be dictated to. He had decreed that Anne Boleyn's daughter Elizabeth was to succeed him if they failed to produce a son. Henry publicly rebuked Cromwell. Cromwell, thwarted by Anne both at home and abroad, was alienated from both her and the powerful Boleyn faction at court.

Despite these background facts Cromwell's true motivations remain a mystery. But what is certain is that sometime early in 1536 Cromwell decided to move against Anne, accusing her of adultery and treason. In one ruthless action, he engineered both her demise and much of the Boleyn faction at court, and thus consolidated his own power base. Cranmer was stunned. He had been kept away from Henry during the days before Anne's trial, so he had to resort to writing a letter. Wanting to plead her innocence while at the same time not wanting (or daring) to criticize the king or his actions, he wrote:

> *I am in such a perplexity, that my mind is clearly amazed; for I never had better opinion in woman, than I had in her; which maketh me to think, that she should not be culpable.*

Some have seen the letter as a weak attempt by Cranmer to ingratiate himself with Henry at the same time as saving face with the Boleyn faction. But by the standard of the day Cranmer was being extraordinarily bold. MacCulloch says, 'Cranmer's negotiation of a frightening and complex situation is a model of pastoral wisdom and courage.'

Cranmer annuls Anne's marriage

Nonetheless, Cranmer bowed to the inevitable and visited Anne in the Tower on 16 May. Some sort of deal had been done whereby Anne would confess, and there would be a declaration by Cranmer the next day that her marriage to Henry was null. There was a remarkable illogicality at the centre of all this: if Anne's marriage to Henry was no marriage, she could not have committed adultery, so in turn she could not be guilty of treason. But Cranmer complied with the whole charade and saw his friend, chief supporter, and the person who had looked to him for spiritual guidance go to her death. On the day of her execution, he could not bear to be present, instead he wept bitterly in the gardens at Lambeth Palace. In a life marked by compromise this whole episode stands out as particularly damaging to Cranmer's integrity. But even here it should be pointed out that Anne herself might have asked Cranmer to play his part. Anne knew her fate was inevitable. But her daughter, Elizabeth, not yet three years old, was also vulnerable — Anne knew how ruthless Henry could be to ensure he got the succession to the throne he wanted. If she accepted that her marriage was null and got the Primate of the newly independent church to declare such, Elizabeth's claim to the throne would be substantially weakened; her daughter would then not be seen as such a threat to Catherine's daughter Mary — or any subsequent child Henry might have. Was Cranmer prepared to go along with this, having risked his own position to save her, but now knowing there was nothing more he could do? The weeping in that case was for a fellow believer's fate and not for any lack of courage he had displayed during her downfall.

The *Ten Articles*

Despite Anne's death the evangelical cause was not lost. Cromwell, for his part in paving the way for Henry to marry the new object of his desire, Jane Seymour, was duly rewarded with the office of Lord Privy Seal and granted a peerage. He had gained power in the church's break from Rome, and he had no intention of letting those at court sympathetic to papal claims gain ascendancy. So the confusing theological mix continued: when Convocation opened on 9 June 1536, Mass was celebrated, but Latimer preached two sermons to the gathered clergy attacking clerical immorality and ignorance, the doctrine of purgatory, shrines and devotion to images; he even advocated an increasing use of English in church services.

Convocation now attempted its first definition of what the Church *of* England, rather than the Church *in* England, believed by producing the *Ten Articles* of religion. These were the forerunners to the *Thirty-Nine Articles* that were still in use in the Church of England up into the twentieth century. Significantly, they embraced the Lutheran view of justification that works played no part in a believer's salvation. This is a cornerstone of evangelical belief encapsulated in Ephesians 2:8: 'For by grace you have been saved through faith. And this is not your own doing; it is the gift of God.' Furthermore, to the annoyance of traditionalists, the *Ten Articles* mentioned only three sacraments: baptism, Eucharist and penance. But Cranmer already thought that that was one too many, having previously expressed doubts about the efficacy of auricular confession to a priest.

But the *Ten Articles* were not uniformly evangelical and were only agreed after much wrangling in Convocation, the king himself claiming that he had been forced to resolve the deadlock. Perhaps because of this they were not only the first but the last doctrinal statement put out by Convocation, at least until 1563. All subsequent ones were put together by bishops and theologians in private committees with Convocation having little or no say in them. Furthermore, directions were now given under the authority of the vicegerent without recourse to Convocation, including, in 1537, an instruction that every parish priest should make available a copy of the Bible in Latin and English. But the only complete English Bible was that published by Miles Coverdale — and that was without official approval.

It was at this time also that Cromwell sought to increase his personal wealth by co-opting the income of various church estates for himself, including some allocated for Cranmer, to which Cranmer offered only token resistance. When many smaller monasteries were dispersed in 1536, Cranmer sometimes made claims for them on behalf of relatives or friends, but never for himself.

The Pilgrimage of Grace

Not everybody was happy with the theological direction of travel mapped out in the *Ten Articles*, demonstrated in 1536 by an uprising in the north of England. The rebels' aim was to do away with both Cranmer and Cromwell and to reverse the changes. The Pilgrimage of Grace rebellion lasted into the spring of February 1537 and was a serious threat to Henry's government, but Henry survived with a combination of negotiation and a series of ruthless executions.

The Bishops' Book

In the winter of 1537, a special assembly was called by Cromwell to further consider doctrinal matters. In his opening speech, he said that the king had directed that all arguments should refer to Scripture. Many wanted the four medieval sacraments (confirmation, marriage, priestly orders, and anointing of the sick) that had been omitted from the *Ten Articles* reinstated, but Cranmer did not. He called attention to the key question: whether the outward performance of the sacraments 'doth justify man, or whether we receive our justification through faith'. The assembly duly produced *The Institution of a Christian man*, otherwise known as *The Bishops' Book*. It was a victory for the conservatives in that the four sacraments were reinstated, but Cranmer's party managed to get in a paragraph that pointed out that only baptism, the Eucharist, and penance were instituted by Christ.

Another debate of the age, which might seem surprising, was how many commandments Moses received: was it nine or ten? Early in the Christian era there had been a tradition of combining the first two commandments (to have no other God and no graven images) into one, even arguing that the commandment about the graven images was a late addition. On the Continent, Luther was happy with this tradition (and indeed was never troubled much by images) but Huldrych Zwingli (1484–1531), based in Zurich, was not. It was undoubtedly Cranmer that got the 'Zurich' numbering into *The Bishops' Book*, which in turn laid the path for the destruction of images, a vivid trademark of the Reformation in England. The publication of the book was delayed as the wrangling over the text continued. Henry himself made extensive notes on his copy and asked others, including Cranmer, to comment on them. Cranmer's robust correction of Henry's grammar and theology shows both the close relationship that he had with Henry and his confidence in that. In his comments, Cranmer gave his own English translation of the *Apostles' Creed* that impressed Henry and found its way virtually unaltered into *The Book of Common Prayer*.

But this correspondence also reveals that Henry's heart, at least at this stage, was really with the traditionalists in that he wanted the book to reflect the late medieval view that salvation was a matter of man cooperating with God. Salvation, he said, came 'as long as I persevere in his precepts and laws'. Cranmer stood firm, explaining to the king that works came from faith, and that such faith was not merely intellectual consent but the gift of God to the elect. The mature Cranmer was at one with Calvin on his doctrine of election.

But Cranmer on the whole was not successful in his attempts at modifying the text and *The Bishops' Book* never received royal authority. For Cranmer the reform agenda was always subject to the whims of Henry and resistance from conservative factions at court and within the church. It was at this time that his frustration burst out when he discovered that that year (1537) Henry's court had observed St Lawrence's day. While dictating a routine letter to Cromwell, he took the pen from his secretary's hand and wrote: 'but my Lord, if in the court you do keep such holydays and fasting ... when shall we persuade people to cease from them?'

The Bible in English

At the first convocation over which Cranmer presided in 1534, it had been decided to suggest to the king that trustworthy people should be nominated to undertake a fresh translation of Scripture. Without waiting for a specific royal mandate, Cranmer took an existing version of the New Testament and divided it among the most scholarly of the bishops and others to be corrected and returned to him by a given date. When Bishop Stokesley was asked for his contribution, he replied that he felt it was abusing the people to give them liberty to read the Scriptures, and indeed it 'did nothing else but infect them with heresies'. Before Cranmer's translation team could finish, John Rogers (1500–1555), under the pseudonym Thomas Matthew, having worked on an incomplete translation of Tyndale's, had had the resulting complete text printed in Antwerp. Cranmer received a copy, and in August 1536 he sent it on to the king with a warm commendation. To Cranmer's delight Henry duly approved it and authorized it for general sale.

A royal birth and death

On 12 October 1537, Jane Seymour gave Henry the son for which he had waited so long. Cranmer was named a godparent at Edward's christening three days later. The nation rejoiced, and Cranmer would have done more so had he known at this stage what a powerful force for reform this prince would turn out to be. But the rejoicing was short-lived as Jane herself died just twelve days later.

Cromwell, however, was now at the height of his influence: church services in English were encouraged and clerical marriages openly tolerated (although Cranmer was still discreet about his own). During 1538, many statues and other images were destroyed. It was Cranmer himself who wrote to Cromwell saying that he suspected that at the shrine of his predecessor (Thomas Becket, famously murdered in Canterbury Cathedral in 1170), the display of martyrs' blood be 'but a feigned thing made of some red ochre or of such like matter' and suggested that Cromwell's men might be commissioned 'to try and examine that and all other like things there'.

The mood of the times was reinforced by the execution in May 1538 of the Franciscan friar John Forest who staunchly refused to acknowledge Henry as head of the church in the pope's place. Latimer preached a sermon against idolatry and Cranmer looked on as Forest died in the flames. Latimer certainly thought the evangelical cause had been furthered by this event. Our own mixture of bewilderment, horror and revulsion is a measure of how much Latimer, Cranmer, and others, were children of their time — so we have to be careful about making hasty judgements. But nonetheless, for two men who prided themselves in adhering to Scripture, it seems strange that they could blot out of their minds Christ's injunction to Peter to put away his sword (Matthew 26:50-53), a clear indication that the gospel cause was not to be defended with violence.

A new diplomatic alliance sought

At about this time, the King of France and the Holy Roman Emperor made peace. Henry saw this as a potential threat to

England, and despite a series of offers for marriage alliances in that direction, either for himself or his daughter Mary, he was secretly courting the friendship of the Lutheran princes of Germany and Scandinavia. A delegation of German theologians arrived for discussions with Cranmer and others to see if some doctrinal agreement could be reached, but nothing definite came from this.

Then in September 1538, Stephen Gardiner, a prominent conservative churchman with the ear of the king, arrived in England after three years in France. There followed a proclamation from Henry against clerical marriages, and on 16 November, John Lambert (alias Nicholson), an evangelical activist, was burned. Not all the blame can be laid at Gardiner's door. The sad fact is that Cranmer was party to Lambert's death accusing him, in effect, of believing in the 'spiritual' rather than the 'corporal' presence of Christ in the Eucharist, the latter being the current orthodoxy. At his trial in 1555 Cranmer lamented the irony of this, as later in life he had himself come to embrace Lambert's eucharistic views.

There was a general fear of radicalism at this time, epitomized by the persecution of Anabaptists both in England and on the Continent. When it was pointed out to Cranmer that at times he himself was stricter with those who opposed the teachings of Rome than those that did not, he paraphrased Jesus' comment:

That servant who knows the master's will and does not get ready or does not do what the master wants will be beaten with many blows. But the one who does not know and does things deserving punishment will be beaten with few blows. From everyone who has been given much, much will be

demanded; and from the one who has been entrusted with
much, much more will be asked (Luke 12:47-48).

In any case these events marked, or at least coincided with, the beginning of a new phase. For the rest of Henry's reign (up to within two months of his death) any gains made by evangelicals were precarious and liable to reversal as the theological weather vane swung one way, then another. Battling at the helm of the ship was Archbishop Cranmer, held up to ridicule by both evangelicals and conservatives, for hanging on with such grim determination in the face of every reversal. These criticisms will be considered in the final chapter.

4

THE LATER YEARS WITH HENRY VIII

The Great (alias Cranmer's) Bible

Although the evangelical cause suffered numerous setbacks in the later years of Henry VIII's reign, in April 1539 there appeared the first edition of a new officially authorized Great Bible. This new translation was not, it seems, initiated by Cromwell (as some have claimed), instead Cromwell was prompted by Cranmer to persuade Henry to agree to its publication. Cranmer had given up on his bishops producing the translation that he had asked for, suggesting their work would not be ready until 'the day after doomsday'. On the Great Bible's title page a grateful people receive the word of God from the monarch — on his right the clerics and on his left the lay people. Despite Henry's innate conservatism and fear of radicalism, he seemed genuinely interested in securing the Bible in English for his subjects: he said that he wanted 'free and liberal use of the Bible in our own maternal tongue'. He commissioned Cranmer to write a new preface for the Great Bible, which subsequently gained the misleading designation 'Cranmer's Bible'.

But just at this time Henry, after failing to come to any agreement with the Lutheran princes, decided England's political fortunes lay with an alliance with the Empire after all, which in turn meant demonstrating that at heart he was a true Catholic — his problem all along had apparently been with the papacy.

The *Six Articles*

The *Six Articles* were duly pushed through Parliament the same year; they were undoubtedly a reversal for the evangelical cause. They reaffirmed Communion in one kind, clerical celibacy, the vows of chastity, and restated the doctrine of transubstantiation. Furthermore, they declared that confession is 'expedient and necessary' and that private masses should be permitted. But it was not perhaps as bad as it appeared for evangelicals: the word 'transubstantiation' was not used and confession was not described, as it had been previously, as 'necessary to the law of God'.

Henry knew that the *Six Articles* went against Cranmer's conscience, and so he told his friend that he could miss the final vote on the passage of the bill in the House of Lords. In a similar vein, when Sir John Gostwick complained to Henry about Cranmer's sermons, which it appears were not in accord with the *Articles*, Henry was furious and threatened Gostwick with retribution if he did not personally apologize to Cranmer; no idle threat from one of the most ruthless monarchs of his age. Loyalty to Henry, at least in part, accounts for the fact that Cranmer stayed on as archbishop when others at this time advised him to flee the country. But it is thought that, in 1539, Margaret, Cranmer's German-speaking wife, and at least one child, were sent back home and only returned again sometime under Edward's rule. It is only to be wondered how he had managed to keep her presence secret when so many of Cranmer's enemies were eager to discredit him before the king.

Despite the setback of the *Six Articles* all was not lost for the evangelicals: Henry's decision in the autumn of 1539 to marry Anne of Cleves, the sister of a Saxon prince, indicated a move away from an alliance with Roman Catholic France and the Holy Roman Empire, and instead towards Lutheran Germany. Although Cranmer was part of the negotiating team for this match, he showed his pastoral concern for Henry when he expressed doubts that Anne would make him happy. The politically motivated Cromwell had no time for what he saw as Cranmer's naïve approach and pushed the negotiations through — much to his subsequent regret.

The downfall of Thomas Cromwell

Later in 1539, Henry eventually met Anne of Cleves and immediately felt he had been duped about her supposed beauty. Despite Henry's attempts to avoid the match it was felt the political fallout would be too great and on 6 January 1540, Cranmer performed the ceremony.

But the king never forgave Cromwell. His enemies now saw their chance and plotted against him, with the result that on 10 June, he was arrested and taken to the Tower. As he had three years previously for Anne Boleyn, Cranmer now pleaded heroically Cromwell's hopeless cause. But the conservatives were in the ascendancy, and they had successfully snared their chief enemy: the political genius who for so long had had the ear of the king which had enabled him to ruthlessly push through the reforms they had so resented. On 28 July 1540, Cromwell suffered the same fate as the young Anne Boleyn whom he had so effectively plotted against. And ironically, like her, he was falsely convicted on a confusing mixture of rumour and innuendo. It is said that Henry VIII deliberately chose an inexperienced executioner, a young boy, who made three attempts at severing Cromwell's head before finally succeeding.

What is to be made of Cromwell? Without him the pace of reform would have been less swift and might have stalled altogether. Cranmer did not have the political skill to work in that arena — he relied on Cromwell to push through both Parliament and Convocation all of the changes he wanted. They had a close and successful working relationship and, indeed, friendship. And yet it seems the motivations of the two men were entirely different. Cromwell does not appear to have had a personal faith in the gospel that the new learning had revealed; he backed the reforms in as far as they enhanced his power and wealth, dispensing with others (notably Anne Boleyn) when they got in his way. In contrast, Cranmer used his power in office, an office he was reluctant to accept, to drive forward the cause of the gospel, often at personal cost to himself and eventually, as shall be seen, paying the ultimate price to witness to the Saviour he believed in.

Anne of Cleves divorced

Now there was more controversy for Cranmer as he looked to do Henry's bidding to extract him from the marriage with Anne of Cleves. It was decided that there existed for Anne a pre-contract of marriage with the Duke of Lorraine; this, coupled with Henry's claimed lack of adequate consent and non-consummation, absolved the consciences of a sufficient number of clergy in the gathered assembly to pronounce, on 9 July 1540, that the marriage was null. The anomalies created by the abundance of reasons mustered for the annulment echo the annulment of Anne Boleyn's marriage. Anne of Cleves graciously accepted the divorce and retired to the country on a generous pension from Henry. MacCulloch wryly comments: 'No one has ever suggested she made the wrong decision.' Within days Henry had married the nineteen-year-old Catherine Howard.

The Privy Council formalized

To sum up the confusion of these tumultuous times, on 30 July, Henry executed for treason three Catholics who supported the papacy, and three prominent evangelicals for heresy. The following month the Privy Council, which up to this point had been an informal group of advisors to the king, was given a formal constitution. First in the list of precedence was to be the Archbishop of Canterbury.

But Henry's health was in decline, and he often expressed his regret at Cromwell's demise; he seems to have realized, somewhat belatedly, that the charges against him had largely been false. Henry realized that he needed to be wary of those at court whose allegiance was primarily to Rome and the old religion. Furthermore, unrest continued in the north of the country and this reminded the king of how close the earlier Pilgrimage of Grace had been to becoming a major rebellion. Neither of these facts did the evangelical cause any harm and when the king went on a visit to the north with his new wife Catherine Howard, Cranmer was left behind very much 'in charge' of the affairs of state. In May, the Privy Council announced financial penalties for parishes that did not have a copy of the Great Bible in every church. The French ambassador who, understandably, was having difficulty keeping his bearings with the theological seesaw, reported back with some amazement to King Francis that in England preaching was now to be based on the pure text of Scripture. In July, Cranmer was the author of a royal proclamation reducing the number of saints' days and, in the autumn, royal letters were sent out ordering the final destruction of the remaining shrines, including the image of Our Lady at Canterbury Cathedral.

The Six Preachers

Furthermore, Cranmer was able to ensure the appointment of several evangelical clergy to vacant posts, including three of the Six Preachers of Canterbury Cathedral. One, John Scory, reportedly preached at the cathedral in March 1541 that 'he that doth deny that only faith doth justify would deny, if he durst be so bold, that Christ doth justify'. Many cathedral staff made formal complaints to Cranmer, but he gave them short shrift: 'You make a band, do you? I will break your band, ywis, and I will make you leave your mumpsimus.'[1] Cranmer had always wanted the cathedral to be a place of learning, like a university college, but the conservatives wanted it to be a place of prayer and beautiful music; it could be that Cranmer had some residual anger with the cathedral staff over losing that battle. The conservative view on the role of cathedrals within the Anglican Church has prevailed down to our own day.

On 1 June of the same year, Cranmer went to the cathedral and had an argument with Serles, one of the three conservative Six Preachers (Henry's idea of trying to balance the theological seesaw), over the devotion to images. In September, Serles took his complaints about Cranmer direct to Henry who was then in York; he was not granted an audience but members of the council with the king sent Serles back with a letter to Cranmer that Serles was not allowed to open. On receipt of the letter Cranmer had Serles committed to prison and temporarily expelled from the Six Preachers, thus demonstrating that in his stand against images Cranmer had support from within the council.

Catherine Howard's demise

It was at this time that Catherine Howard's sexual immorality before marriage and her subsequent adultery with Thomas Culpeper came to light. A minor courtier, John Lascelles, an evangelical, had been told by his sister what others at court already knew; Lascelles in turn chose to tell Cranmer. Cranmer shared the information with his co-councillors, Audley and Hertford, who had been left in London like Cranmer while the king and queen were on their royal visit in the north. Audley and Hertford decided, not surprisingly, that it was Cranmer and not themselves who should present the news to Henry on his return. But even Cranmer, with his close friendship with the king, did not have the courage to speak the words to the face of the notoriously volcanic Henry and instead handed him a letter as the king attended Mass on 2 November 1541. Henry was stunned. But Cranmer need not have feared; his friendship and pastoral skill seemed to have prevented an immediate explosion of wrath from the king. This time there was no intricate fabricated plot. It emerged that, despite only being a young teenager, she had lived a sexually immoral life while living with the dowager Duchess of Norfolk (seemingly with that lady's knowledge) and had continued such while married to Henry. It was Cranmer who interviewed Catherine and despite initially denying the charges she eventually admitted to them all. Catherine's lovers were executed in the December and Catherine herself in February 1542, along with her chief accomplice Lady Rochford — Anne Boleyn's sister-in-law. At Anne Boleyn's trial Lady Rochford (Jane Boleyn), never a sympathizer with the evangelical cause, had falsely accused Anne and her own husband, George (also an evangelical), of incest. It is said that Jane declared her own death to be God's just punishment on her for the false accusations she had made against George and Anne.

Proposed revisions to the Great Bible

Many conservative members in Convocation had never been happy about making a Bible in English available in the parishes. But when, in January 1542, it was decided to give Convocation the task of revising the Great Bible, those sympathetic to the conservative cause were keen to influence any new translation, and so they embraced the opportunity. Gardiner himself financed the distribution of an existing volume to enable those of their number considered to be theologians to start work. But in March Cranmer announced, much to the consternation of Convocation, that it was the king's wish that the universities should undertake the revision instead. But the Great Bible was in any case safe, as shortly after the announcement a royal four-year monopoly was given to Anthony Marler to print the existing version. In the end, there was no new official version until Elizabeth's reign.

The King's Book

In April 1543, Convocation sought to provide a new doctrinal statement based on a revision of the original *Bishops' Book*. In the debates, despite Cranmer's ever more desperate pleas, including an appeal to Henry to intercede, the doctrine of justification by faith was rejected. Published in the May and titled *The Necessary Doctrine and Erudition for any Christian Man*, it became known as *The King's Book*. Henry had demonstrated, as he had in his marginal notes on the original *Bishops' Book* deliberations, that he could not shake off the traditional teaching of the church — that of a works-based salvation. It undoubtedly represented a setback for the evangelicals.

Henry pushed on with his reversals of the reforms, probably because he wanted to show Charles V, to whom he was making diplomatic overtures, that at heart he was an

orthodox Roman Catholic. There followed a parliamentary
bill to prohibit from Bible reading any group below the social
standing of a yeoman (usually a free man owning a small
area of land). In turn leading evangelicals were rounded
up and detained for questioning as the conservative forces
in London and Canterbury sensed things at last were
going their way. Undoubtedly Stephen Gardiner, Bishop of
Winchester, was a moving force behind this.

Henry marries Catherine Parr

On 12 July 1543, Henry married his final wife Catherine Parr.
Within days of the marriage the Privy Council, in Cranmer's
absence, authorized the burning of three evangelicals at
Windsor. Henry was keeping his distance from Cranmer
during these theological reversals. For example, he had not
been asked to officiate at the royal wedding ceremony.

Although it seems that Catherine was initially
conservative in her beliefs, under Cranmer's influence she
moved to an evangelical position during the short time
she was married to Henry. This is clearly evidenced in the
book that she wrote and had published shortly after Henry's
death, which proclaimed justification by faith alone.

An archbishop in danger

Notwithstanding any evangelical teaching the new queen
might have already embraced, this was an especially
dangerous time for Cranmer. The conservatives were in
the ascendancy again, Bishop Gardiner being a particularly

determined and powerful enemy of the evangelicals. In April 1543, a report of heresy in Kent (where Canterbury Cathedral is situated) was brought before the Privy Council. The council in turn presented the case to the king. The finger of blame was pointed directly at Cranmer himself. The summer wore on and a head of steam built up against Cranmer, but Henry did not seem to be taking any action. Then one late summer evening, as Henry was enjoying a trip down the Thames in his royal barge accompanied by his musicians, he came to Lambeth Bridge and called out to Cranmer: 'Ah, my chaplain, I have news for you! I know now who is the greatest heretic in Kent.' Henry duly showed the documentary evidence to Cranmer who 'besought his Highness to appoint such commissioners as would effectually try out the truth of those articles'. Henry told the hapless Cranmer that there was indeed to be an enquiry, only it was to be Cranmer himself who was going to be chief investigator; what is more he was to choose whosoever he wanted to assist him in his investigation. The greatest heretic in Kent was to investigate and pass judgement on himself.

Henry was a ruthless king and he could be petty and vindictive to those to whom he owed much. His friendship and loyalty to Cranmer in every phase of their shared life must surely speak much of Cranmer himself. Cranmer could now act against those that had not only sought to disgrace him but also, by their actions, had done so much to hinder the cause of the gospel. But Cranmer's investigation lacked rigour; MacCulloch comments that Cranmer 'had repeatedly shown himself devoid of the killer instinct if there was no one to back him up'. Or perhaps we could say when Cranmer was acting alone and not being pressured by somebody else's agenda, he was happier to turn the other cheek. Cranmer allowed his commission of investigation to drag on with no definitive result. As a consequence, the conservatives began to regroup and two leading evangelicals were indicted for their preaching. On seeing the danger, and on Henry's authority, Ralph Morice, Cranmer's personal secretary, co-opted the more ruthless Dr Thomas Legh onto the enquiry team. Surprise night raids on prominent conservatives revealed incriminating correspondence. But Cranmer, after berating the culprits, duly forgave them and even continued to rely on some for their services, subsequently appointing one of them as a bishop.

Cranmer had yet to face one last attempt to bring him down; this time it was the Privy Council itself that plotted against him. It could be that the councillors wanted Cranmer out of the way before his commission of enquiry got to them. At the end of November 1543, they sought permission from Henry to summon Cranmer to appear and hear a fresh set of heresy charges put to him. Henry duly agreed but forewarned Cranmer in a private meeting of what was afoot. It seems that Cranmer thought he could successfully defend himself, to which the king replied: 'Do you not think that if they have you once in prison, three or four false knaves will soon be procured to witness against you and condemn you?' Then Henry gave Cranmer his personal ring.

Cranmer appeared next day at the council but was kept waiting outside for nearly an hour. When finally summoned inside, his colleagues duly announced that he was under arrest. Cranmer's response was simply to show them the ring, a sign that he had the personal protection and authority of the king behind him. Rushing from the chamber to escape the scene of a possible disaster they were met by Henry. Morice (Cranmer's personal secretary) tells the story:

'How [asks Henry] have ye handled here my Lord Canterbury? What, make ye of him a slave, shutting him out of the Council chamber amongst serving men? ... I would you should well understand, that I account my Lord of Canterbury as faithful a man towards me as ever was prelate in this realm, and one to whom I am many ways beholding, by the faith, I owe unto God ... and therefore whoso will loveth me will regard him thereafter.' Upon this speech, they all, and especially the Duke of Norfolk, offered an excuse. They meant no harm to the Archbishop by putting him in the Tower; they thought that after his trial he would be set at liberty to his greater glory ... And so the King departed and the Lords shook hands every man with my Lord Cranmer, against whom nevermore after no man durst spurn during the King Henry's life.

Cranmer was safe. A consequence of the failed coup was that two were arrested: one died in prison, one was executed. Cranmer, true to form, showed no thirst for revenge or any malice and actually acted as a patron for one of those pardoned — the writer John Heywood.

In December 1543, the archbishop's palace at Canterbury was destroyed by fire, and Cranmer's brother-in-law and others died in the flames. The following August, when French warships threatened to make a landing at Dover, Cranmer (an accomplished hunter and rider) appeared on horseback with a hundred horsemen. He wore a helmet and carried a dagger, a page at his side ready with his gun. It was a striking image strangely at odds with the timid churchman and was long remembered in Kent.

Calmer waters

During the remainder of the 1540s, evangelicals steadily built their influence at court. Aiding the calmer theological waters seems to have been Henry's genuine happiness in his marriage with Catherine Parr. Her growing evangelical convictions must have been a great encouragement to Cranmer as he saw her stepson, Prince Edward, surrounded by tutors with evangelical leanings.

Despite this more benign atmosphere, the last year of Henry's life demonstrated that the evangelical cause still faced difficulties. Cranmer asked Henry to write to him urging him to abolish the adoration of images and crucifixes, but Stephen Gardiner wrote from Brussels warning Henry against further religious changes that might jeopardize negotiations with Charles V. The conservatives at court, despite recent reversals, renewed their efforts, believing the stakes were now higher as Henry's health grew weaker. Anne Askew (1521–1546), an evangelical who had links with Cranmer, was arrested and interrogated under torture by Chancellor Wriothesley and Lord Rich. They were hoping that she might reveal the names of wives of leading figures at court who had evangelical convictions, which, despite repeated efforts on the levers of the infamous rack by these eminent men, she categorically refused to do. She was eventually burnt at the stake on 16 July 1546, with three other evangelicals, including John Lascelles.

In light of the previous thirteen years of strife and rhetoric against Rome, it is a strange historical fact that it was at this time that Henry, in some considerable secrecy, was in touch with Gurone Bertano, a representative of the pope. It appears Henry was seeking some sort of reconciliation with

Rome. Some think that Henry pulled back from this venture because of the plot against Anne Askew. He suspected that Wriothesley and Rich were hoping she would implicate his beloved Queen Catherine.

But in the last months of his life, perhaps under the influence of his wife, Henry seemed to have renewed convictions about the direction of the reforms. In a spat over an exchange of land with the king, Gardiner misjudged Henry's mood, and he was promptly removed from the Privy Council. Another leading conservative, the Earl of Surrey (son of the powerful Duke of Norfolk), was executed.

A dying king

In late January, Henry knew the end was near, and refusing to see any other cleric, he summoned the archbishop. In the early hours of 28 January, Cranmer arrived. Henry was by now unable to speak:

As soon as he came, the King stretched out his hand to him. The Archbishop exhorted him to place all his hope in the mercy of God through Christ, beseeching him earnestly that if he could not testify this hope in words, he would do so by a sign. Then the King wrung the Archbishop's hand, which he held in his own, as hard as his failing strength would allow, and, directly after, breathed his last.

Was this Henry, like the dying thief on the cross, at the last moment putting his complete trust in the Saviour? MacCulloch thinks so:

Quietly playing out his calling as royal chaplain, Cranmer had won a final victory in his years of argument with the King on justification. No last rites for Henry; no extreme unction: just an evangelical statement of faith in a grip of the hand. Thus ended the most long-lasting relationship of love which either man had known.

Some think that Cranmer now grew a beard as a sign of mourning for the king, but more likely it was to identify with the Reformation; on the Continent a clerical beard was a sign of the break with Rome. Certainly for Cranmer a new chapter now opened in his life. He had a new freedom. He no longer had to look over his shoulder to gauge Henry's reaction, and for the first time he was able to publicly acknowledge the presence of his wife and children.

Note

1. 'Ywis' is an old English word meaning 'certainly'. 'Mumpsimus', a word in modern dictionaries, but rarely used, is an obvious error that is obstinately repeated despite correction.

5

A NEW BEGINNING UNDER EDWARD VI

Edward crowned king

On 20 February, the nine-year-old Edward was crowned king — Cranmer specifically making reference to the Old Testament reforming king, Josiah:

> *Your Majesty is God's vice-gerent and Christ's vicar within your own dominions, and to seek, with your predecessor Josiah, God truly worshipped, and idolatry destroyed, the tyranny of the bishops of Rome banished from your subjects, and images removed.*

Cranmer made the point that although Edward had been anointed king by him, it was 'but a ceremony'. Edward was already king:

> *not in respect of the oil which the bishop useth, but in consideration of their power which is preordained ... the*

King is yet a perfect monarch notwithstanding, and God's
anointed, as well as if he was inoiled.

The reform agenda continues

It seemed that there was now little to stop the Reformation
in England moving forward. But Cranmer worried that if the
reform agenda was pushed forward too quickly, people would
see it as a manipulation of a child-king by a Protestant clique,
and popular support would be lost. And with the old king
dead, despite believing (as did Cranmer) in the divine right of
kings to rule the church, Bishop Gardiner, the longstanding
opponent of Cranmer, positioned himself more clearly with
the conservatives and against the reform agenda.

Nonetheless the council issued a set of injunctions in the
young king's name regulating worship in England. Among
other things, they attacked those who practised various
superstitions:

> *In casting holy water upon his bed, upon images, and other*
> *dead things; or bearing about him holy bread, or St John's*
> *Gospel, or making crosses of wood upon Palm Sunday in*
> *time of reading of the passion, or keeping of private holy*
> *days, as bakers, brewers, smiths and shoemakers, and such*
> *others do; or ringing of holy bells, or blessing with the holy*
> *candle, to the intent thereby to be discharged of the burden*
> *of sin, or to bribe away devils, or to put away dreams and*
> *fantasies.*

It was at this time that the heresy legislation was changed.
There is some confusion about the meaning of the new law,

but the effect was to bring executions for heresy under church law at this time to an end. The only two martyrs in Edward's reign, Joan Bocher, an Anabaptist, and George Van Parris, a Unitarian, were put to death under common law.

On 8 March 1547, a royal proclamation announced Parliament's enactment about Communion in both kinds and promised: 'from time to time further official travail for the reformation and setting forth of such godly orders as may be most to God's glory, the edifying of our subjects, and for the advancement of true religion'. The move from 'Mass' to 'Communion' was being put in place; the sacrificial presentation of the bread and wine was officially a thing of the past. By the time Parliament had ended in March 1549, the English Church was ready to adopt a liturgy totally in English (the new English-language *Prayer Book* became compulsory on 9 June), the clergy could marry, and the Archbishop of Canterbury had openly declared a Reformed view of the Eucharist.

Social unrest

In the country, it was perceived that the pace of change was accelerating. Eamon Duffy comments that the Marian church-wardens of Stanford articulated a generally shared perception when they said, 'The tyme of Scysme when this Realm was devyded from the Catholic Churche ... [was the] second yer of Kyng Edward the syxt'.

There was certainly widespread social unrest and a rebellion in the West Country was triggered by the religious reforms. In one particular instance, Walter Raleigh (the father of the famous seaman), when riding to Exeter, criticized a woman he saw carrying rosary beads. The old woman hurried on to her church to attend Mass where the gathered parishioners were enraged to hear of Raleigh's comments. In the subsequent uprising large numbers lost their lives.

Despite this, the new *Prayer Book* (thought to be substantially the work of Cranmer) was seen as evolutionary; a temporary measure, on the road to what he perceived as a truly evangelical liturgy. But many bishops were not happy with the direction of travel, evidenced by the restoration in the 1549 *Prayer Book* of the previously abandoned word 'Mass', even though the substance of the liturgy was now 'Communion'. In other words, the emphasis in the new *Prayer Book* service was on the participation by believers in a memorial festival rather than a sacrificial representation of the body and blood of Christ. The new *Prayer Book* retained some saints' days but removed the idea of the intercession of saints. It also included a newly worded marriage service still used by some today.

One outcome of Cranmer's changing beliefs and his rewriting of the liturgy of the church was that it began to highlight the changing concept of the church minister. The Eucharist service had now shifted the focus from the minister, the priest who called down Christ into the elements, to the recipient, the Christian in the pew. The Eucharist was still considered the central act of worship in the church, but the balance had now changed. Furthermore, as Cranmer believed in the doctrine of election, the emphasis again was not on the relationship of the believer to the priest, but the relationship of the believer to his Saviour. A related and unresolved question at this time was: were ministers of the church the ministers of the Crown or the ministers of Christ? This question caused Cranmer some difficulties when Mary ascended the throne and began to reverse the reform agenda.

Tension among evangelicals about the pace of reform

Despite the rapidity of the changes that had infuriated conservative churchmen some, including émigrés such as Martin Bucer of Strasbourg (who had been appointed Regius Professor of Divinity at the University of Cambridge), felt the reforms were not going fast enough or far enough. In particular Bucer was not happy about the retention of vestments (special garments worn for different parts of the liturgy). Bucer felt vulnerable because some of his continental colleagues were criticizing him for associating with these compromises; he commented:

> Let those who falsely attack because I am here where something of the old leaven is retained, consider how true charity prescribes brothers to be judged, and also that without charity we are nothing.

But the very fact that some of those who complained loudest were émigrés (they had had to flee their home country because of their radical views) was evidence enough for Cranmer that his cautious approach was the right one. But Bucer was not alone. In a sermon in London, John Hooper (*c.* 1500–1555) criticized the retention of the vestments saying that they were 'rather the habit and vesture of Aaron and the gentiles, than of the ministers of Christ'.

Despite clashes with Cranmer, Hooper was nominated to be Bishop of Gloucester. But he was not happy about the mention of saints in the Oath of Supremacy which he was to be compelled to swear on taking office in the church. Cranmer could see that the retention of a reference to saints was anachronistic to the concept of a Reformed liturgy, but he was reluctant to change the specific wording of the oath chosen by Henry. The issue was resolved on the very day of Hooper's formal confirmation in the presence of the thirteen-year-old King Edward on 20 July 1551. Somebody pointed out the wording of the oath to the young king who simply reached forward and crossed out the offending words with his own pen. In one stroke the months of agonizing by Cranmer about how to deal with the issue were over.

Hooper was triumphant, but nonetheless he had agreed the previous February (after being put under enormous pressure) to wear, at the ceremony, the vestments he so disliked. Cranmer's stand on vestments was part of an ongoing fear of radicalism that in his perception might destabilize the country. It was a fear shared by many evangelicals. So it was that in the following May Cranmer endorsed the burning at the stake of Joan Bocher (Joan of Kent) who was perceived to have heretical views about the divine and human natures of Christ. Nonetheless the incident with Hooper portrays the other side of Cranmer: he seemed unable to bear a grudge and could maintain friendships with people he sharply disagreed with when he considered the essentials of the faith were not at stake. He forgave Hooper, and when Hooper wrote to Heinrich Bullinger (1504–1575) shortly after the vestments affair, he referred to Cranmer in the warmest terms and subsequently stayed with Cranmer at Lambeth for three months.

The Stranger Church

It was at this time (July 1551) that a 'Stranger Church' was set up to accommodate the estimated five thousand Protestant refugees from the Netherlands and France now living in London — some ten per cent of the city's population. The motivation was probably, at least in part, to 'ring fence' the more radical evangelicals who had been expelled from the Continent and to give them their own disciplined structure. The superintendent was John Laski (from Poland), a great friend and ally of Hooper. Laski had a free hand (somewhat like John Calvin had had in Geneva), and to the delight of Hooper, he swept away all the 'baggage' (as Laski and Hooper saw it) that had been inherited from the Roman Church. They soon became noted for their lively devotional and intellectual life. The Stranger Church offered an alternative vision for the Church of England: a church cast away from its roots in Rome. But Cranmer was not well pleased and there was correspondence on many of the issues raised, not least on such arcane matters (as it might seem to us now) as whether it was appropriate to stand or sit in the Communion service. But the fundamental issue for Cranmer was: by what authority were these things done? To proceed by due process and popular consent was more important for him than to simply pursue ideological purity as Laski and Hooper had.

Cranmer, Gardiner and the Eucharist

1551 also brought the trial and imprisonment of Stephen Gardiner for disobedience to royal commandments. About this time Cranmer wrote *Defence of the True and Catholic Doctrine of the Sacrament of the Body and Blood of Christ,* where he appears to articulate a position close to that held by the Swiss Reformer Zwingli. He says, 'Figuratively Christ is in the bread and wine, and spiritually He is in them that worthily eat and drink the bread and wine.' In other words, Cranmer, having denied that Christ is in the elements in any real physical way, seems to be saying that Christ is not even present in the elements spiritually, but only in the believer when he worthily partakes of the same. Gardiner wrote an attack on this but cleverly played in the 1549 *Prayer Book* to his argument, managing to establish therein a much more conservative eucharistic doctrine. Cranmer had already decided on a revision of the *Prayer Book* before Gardiner's sharp legal mind had found alternative interpretations, but he decided that Gardiner's comments needed a specific denial and so published *An answer to a crafty and sophistical cavillation devised by Stephen Gardiner.*

Although Cranmer seemed a naturally mild-mannered and polite man, in print he could be cutting and sarcastic — this was in part the spirit of the age (some of Luther's written work seems fairly shocking to modern readers). In *An answer*, Cranmer appealed to the Church Fathers and derided Gardiner's lack of knowledge of such. It was certainly an area in which Cranmer was very knowledgeable. It was not so much that he thought that the Church Fathers and Scripture were of equal authority, but he hoped that if he could demonstrate that the Church Fathers held views close to his own, then it would bolster his position. Unfortunately for the Reformed cause, as MacCulloch points out, 'realist language ... was clearly so common in patristic discussion of the eucharist'. In other words, the language of the Church

Fathers, on the surface at least, appeared to support the Roman position of a real presence in the elements of the service which they called the Mass.

The *Forty-Two Articles* and the 1552 *Prayer Book*

In December 1551, Cranmer began work on three projects: a revision of canon law, a clear doctrinal statement (which eventually emerged as the *Forty-Two Articles*), and a revision of the *Prayer Book*, for which Gardiner's clever reinterpretation had demonstrated the need. Furthermore, Cranmer wanted to see all the evangelical churches in Europe drawn together under England's leadership to agree upon a common canon law; to that end he sent out invitations to Bullinger in Zurich, Calvin in Geneva, and Melanchthon in Wittenberg. Laski from the Stranger's Church in London and John Hooper from Gloucester had already been co-opted, once more demonstrating Cranmer's ability to not let past differences interfere with the progress of the gospel or personal friendship. The hoped-for international commission did not come about, not least because of the difficulties envisaged in having one written canon law to embrace such diverse communities. However, the new *Prayer Book* was authorized in April 1552 and the *Forty-Two Articles* were issued in June 1553, although not formally approved by Convocation.

It was in the Eucharist service of the new *Prayer Book* that Cranmer sought to move ever further away from the Roman Church's concept of transubstantiation. He was making it clear that the gospel words ('This is my body... ') were there to instruct, not to effect any change in the elements; there is no mention of their consecration and at the end of the service the curate is free to take home what is left and use it as ordinary bread and wine. More than a hundred years later, in 1662, a further revision of the *Prayer Book* (the version that has survived into the twentieth century) pulled back from this strongly evangelical stance and stipulated that the elements should be consumed in the church by the 'priest'. Another blow Cranmer looked to strike for the evangelical cause in the 1552 *Prayer Book* was to exclude the possibility of prayers for the dead. Among the changes was the removal of the Eucharist from the funeral service so breaking any sense of continuing communion between the living and the dead which had been such a feature of medieval Roman Catholicism. For many, the practice of saying Mass to ease the deceased's way through purgatory (and often receiving payment for the same from grieving relatives) was one of the chief corruptions of the gospel by the Church of Rome. MacCulloch comments that 'The Church had surrendered its power over death back to the Lord of life and death in heaven', where, as most evangelicals today would see it, it had always belonged.

In 1552, the new *Prayer Book* must have appeared radical to many — but Peter Martyr wrote to Martin Bucer that he felt Cranmer was still being hampered by conservative forces in its production and, later, other evangelicals exiled under Mary expressed the view that if Cranmer had had a free hand he would have moved the Church of England more towards the Stranger Church model in London or that of Calvin's in Geneva.

6

A Reformation halted under Mary I

The death of King Edward

There had been dissent and uprisings for the last five years as the religious changes had been pushed through, but as the summer of 1552 approached and the young King Edward neared manhood, he embarked on his first royal progress through Hampshire, Sussex and Surrey. A new calmer period seemed to have been ushered in. But it was the calm before the storm — that winter Edward's health started to fail and by the following July he was dead.

Even before that cataclysmic event there was a problem with the new *Prayer Book* which was in the process of being printed. The famous Scottish preacher John Knox (*c.* 1514–1572), at the invitation of the Duke of Northumberland, visited London and expressed his surprise at the practice of kneeling at Communion, much to the delight of the Stranger Church. The upshot was that the Privy Council ordered the printers to stop work while the situation was reviewed.

Cranmer was not pleased: 'If such men should be heard, although the book were made every year anew, yet should it not lack faults in their opinion.' Knox and his colleagues failed to force the change, but the *Prayer Book* did carry a note explaining that kneeling did not denote adoration or a real presence, that the elements remained 'in their very natural substances', and that 'the natural body and blood of our Saviour Christ' remained in heaven, 'for it is against the truth of Christ's true natural body to be in more places than in one at one time'. Despite later attribution to Knox this was actually Cranmer's own explanation. This episode demonstrated again Cranmer's fear of radicalism and his resolve that due process must sanction any change and this usually meant parliamentary approval.

Lady Jane Grey

Meanwhile, the king's health had deteriorated and on 11 April 1553, he was moved from London to Greenwich; by May the Privy Council was told by his doctors of the seriousness of the situation. Edward's successor, under the terms of Henry VIII's will, was Mary, his daughter by Catherine of Aragon. It was clear even at this stage that she would turn against evangelicals and look to move the nation back to the Church of Rome, although the ferocity with which she did this could not have been foreseen. To forestall this, it was decided by Edward and his Privy Council that Lady Jane Grey (Edward's first cousin once removed) should marry the son of the Duke of Northumberland (a prominent Privy Councillor) and that she should be nominated by Edward to be his successor. Edward signed his will on 17 June 1553 to that effect.

Attached were several provisions, one of which stated that the executors were 'not to suffer any piece of religion to be altered' and that 'they shall diligently travail to cause godly ecclesiastical laws to be made and set forth, such as may be agreeable with the reformation of religion now received within our realm'. Cranmer was certainly absent when this scheme was devised and his later testimony, which there is no reason to doubt, was that he was a very reluctant convert to it. But King Edward was adamant about the new succession plan, the Privy Council was unanimous, and the legal opinion they had consulted had in turn unanimously endorsed its legitimacy; it was Cranmer alone that stood out against the scheme. Acknowledging that he was no legal expert, at some point between 17 and 19 June, he signed an agreement with other councillors to uphold the new will and its provisions, which diverted the succession to the throne away from Elizabeth, the daughter of the evangelical Anne Boleyn, no less than Mary.

Although in retrospect the scheme appears a bizarre and ill-fated venture, it was not without some logic. Henry VIII had by an Act of Succession diverted the throne away from Mary and Elizabeth to Edward, so why couldn't Edward in turn divert his own succession? And certainly the transfer of power from Henry to Edward had gone through relatively smoothly. Cranmer's consent to all this might be seen as a mistake, but it was certainly not a moral lapse. It was all apiece with his concept of the divine right of kings.

Edward's death came sooner than expected on 6 July. Nevertheless the legalities were all in place and the proclamation went out declaring Lady Jane as Queen. Bishop Nicholas Ridley (c. 1500–1555), a leading evangelical, preached two sermons from his cathedral in London pointing out that Edward's half-sisters, who many thought had a prior claim to the throne, were in fact illegitimate children of Henry. A letter from the Privy Council dated 11 July reaffirmed this view, stating that Henry's divorce from Catherine of Aragon was 'necessary to be had both by the everlasting laws of God, and also by the ecclesiastical laws, and by the most part of the noble and learned the Universities of Christendom', a reference again to the arguments about Leviticus 18:16. But not all were persuaded by the argument when it was first put forward or now on Edward's death. The day might have been carried for Lady Jane if Mary had been detained by the government and kept out of the picture. But on Edward's death she fled to East Anglia and managed to garner popular support.

On 12 July, Cranmer's name headed a circular that ordered the sheriffs of England to gather troops against Mary saying she was plotting to bring into the realm 'papists, Spaniards and other strangers to the great peril and danger of the utter subversion of God's holy word'. But within days news was coming into the capital of the seriousness of the uprising against the new succession. Some Privy Councillors, sensing the game was up, slipped away from the capital, but Cranmer stayed on. He was committed to Lady Jane, even sending some of his own retinue to support the Duke of Northumberland's expedition against Mary and her supporters.

Mary proclaimed queen

However, the popular uprising proved unstoppable and Mary was proclaimed queen on 20 August. Bishop Ridley and other supporters of Lady Jane were arrested and taken to the Tower of London. But Cranmer was still at liberty. He was still Primate of all England, and it was not at all certain to Mary's supporters how any transition back to papal jurisdiction and Roman Catholicism might be put into effect, if there was not some legitimate authority in place. The anomaly of the situation was highlighted when it was realized there was no legal mechanism for imprisoning prominent evangelicals, who boldly continued the attack on 'pestilent popery idolatry and superstition', as did John Rogers in a sermon from the open-air pulpit at St Paul's Cathedral in London. Even the Mayor of London was brave enough to complain about the continuing celebration of the Mass; the newly proclaimed Queen Mary had to make a show of imprisoning the offending priest.

So it was that Cranmer continued in office and presided at the funeral of Edward VI in Westminster Abbey on 8 August. Mary was gracious enough to allow her brother to be buried according to the rights of the *Prayer Book* that he loved, and so he went to his grave at the Abbey with none of the Catholic ceremony that had accompanied the burial of his father. Mary could not face attending it herself and instead staged three days of requiems in the Tower of London where Stephen Gardiner, Cranmer's old enemy, was the celebrant.

But Mary refused to see Cranmer, and he must have known his days were numbered. Despite this he found the time and courage to make pleas for others (for example, Lord Russell and John Cheke) who had been involved in the attempt to divert the throne. MacCulloch says, 'Dignified self-assertion is the keynote of Cranmer's actions in late summer and early autumn 1553. When criticisms are made of cowardice or timidity in his life, the significance of his actions during that period should be remembered.' MacCulloch supports his contention by pointing out that Cranmer could have done what so many did and flee to the Continent. Indeed this was his advice to Jane Wilkinson, a former silkswoman of Anne Boleyn. He wrote to her pointing out that 'Christ, when his hour was not yet come, departed out of his country into Samaria, to avoid the malice of the scribes and Pharisees ... that you will do, do it with speed, lest by your own folly you fall into the persecutors' hands.' Jane did as recommended and had a fruitful ministry encouraging other evangelicals at home and abroad.

Cranmer appeals to the people

As August progressed, Mary gained confidence and issued a proclamation which was seen as giving royal authority to celebrate the Mass. The Duke of Northumberland, whose son had married Lady Jane and was a key player in that coup, succumbed to the mounting pressure and went to Mass. Such high-profile defections among the lay leadership of the country emboldened Mary to take further steps against the evangelical religious leaders. An obvious target was Cranmer, who decided in early September to make public a statement against the Mass and for the *Prayer Book*, which he declared to be 'more pure and according to God's Word than any other that hath been used in England this thousand years'. He had intended to fix the statement, authorized with his personal seal, on every church door in London, but this had been pre-empted when a friend copied it and had it published, probably without Cranmer's permission.

The document caused a sensation in London and was an enormous boost to the beleaguered evangelical cause. It is difficult not to see that Cranmer was trying, Luther-like, to appeal directly to the people and bypass the queen and the council. It was a remarkable step for our cautious sixty-four-year-old archbishop who had always wanted to proceed by due process and with the specific permission of his 'Christian prince'. One wonders if Cranmer had lived longer whether he would have embraced a more radical position and, as some Reformers had, ignored the powers-that-be if he thought that a scriptural principle was at stake.

Cranmer arrested

Not surprisingly the government was less enthusiastic than the crowds in London, and they saw it as a clear case of sedition. Cranmer was summoned before the Privy Council where he faced new councillors, old enemies, and former colleagues who had once more embraced the old religion. He was passed over to a Royal Commission for examination and was there offered an escape path if he would say that his paper against the Mass had been for private publication only; but this he categorically refused to do. The next day Cranmer had dinner with Peter Martyr, a prominent evangelical theologian, and he successfully urged him to get a passport and flee to the Continent as soon as possible. Cranmer knew the outlook for himself and all like-minded people was bleak, but still he refused to take his own advice, although he sent his wife (and probably his children) to Germany; they had to leave secretly and illegally. Cranmer, as has been seen, did not see a flight to escape persecution as

incompatible with Christian obedience; he didn't see martyrdom as the only Christian solution to the dilemma that
many faced at this time. It was the last time he saw his wife
or Peter Martyr. Within days Cranmer's intransigence before the Royal Commission paid its dividend; he was sent to
the Tower, joining Hugh Latimer and Nicholas Ridley there.

And so Cranmer was removed from the centre of political
life and in his absence his own annulment of the Aragon
marriage, dating back to Henry's marriage to Anne Boleyn,
was overturned. The new regime pressed on with its agenda
and for the first time people were described consciously
as 'Catholic' or 'Protestant' rather than conservative or
evangelical.

Cranmer charged with treason

Cranmer was called to stand trial for treason on 13
November 1553 on charges of helping Lady Jane in her
attempt to seize the throne. Along with others so charged
he was made to walk at the head of a procession from the
Tower into the city. He was the only one of the defendants
to plead not guilty; his justification for this can be seen in a
letter he wrote to Queen Mary claiming that in the matter of
the succession he was simply acting on Edward VI's wishes.
Certainly obedience to the sovereign had been Cranmer's
consistent position in his time as archbishop; but under
pressure Cranmer didn't hold to this defence and eventually
pleaded guilty. All five defendants were found guilty and
condemned to death. His possessions were sold off and his
substantial library broken up. In view of his habit of making
detailed notes on the pages of books he read, it is a loss to

scholarship that virtually none of the books by evangelical authors which he is known to have owned have survived.

One can only imagine Cranmer's psychological state at this time. For at least a month after the trial (not to mention the two months before) he had been confined to a cell without air or exercise. He was expecting to be taken out and, in the gaze of the public, to be hung, taken down before dead, disembowelled, to have his limbs amputated, and then to be beheaded. The punishment was for treason, a crime that horrified Cranmer, who throughout his life, often at great personal cost, had looked to obey his monarch.

But Mary was keen that Cranmer should stand trial for what in her mind was a far more serious crime — heresy. While the legalities of this were sorted out (it seemed there was some difficulty charging a man who in the eyes of the law was already dead), Cranmer chose to write to the queen to ask for an interview to discuss the religious changes she was enacting, namely the repudiation of all done in the name of her half-brother Edward VI. He said, 'If I have uttered, I say, my mind unto your Majesty, then I shall think myself discharged.' It seems what Cranmer wanted to do was to voice objection to the new direction of religious policy directly to the monarch; having done so his conscience would be clear, and he could go along with any changes that the new sovereign implemented. Cranmer was certainly bold in his correspondence to the queen, pointing out how harmful to the Crown were the claims of the pope and, in a subsequent letter, pointing out the anomaly of Mary's two coronation oaths, one of obedience to the pope and another to the realm of England. He wrote: 'I fear me that there be contradictions in your oaths, and that those which should have informed your Grace thoroughly, did not their duties therein. If your Majesty ponder the two oaths diligently, I think you shall see you were deceived.' But this was as ever the consistent Cranmer obedient to his sovereign: 'To private subjects it appertaineth not to reform things, but quietly to suffer that they cannot amend.' This did not of course mean that his own evangelical convictions had changed or would change, and surely Mary knew as much.

Cranmer charged with heresy

From 17 December Cranmer was permitted to walk in the garden of the Tower, and perhaps he thought he would be treated more leniently than he had expected. He soon learned that Mary had decided to try him for heresy, and he was to be granted a public disputation of his doctrine. Undoubtedly, Cranmer would have received this news gladly. He was going to be tried for his life's work and not put to death for a crime he did not feel he had committed.

In January, because of overcrowding at the Tower, by happy coincidence, Cranmer shared accommodation with Nicholas Ridley and John Bradford (1510–1555). They were soon joined by Hugh Latimer who later commented: 'There did we together read over the New Testament with great deliberation and painful study.' Cranmer, Ridley and Latimer were seen as key targets by the new Catholic establishment. If they could be discredited doctrinally it would be seen by the public at large as a defeat of the Protestant cause. On 8 March 1554 they were taken from the Tower to Bocardo, a prison in Oxford. Oxford University (unlike Cambridge University) had not embraced evangelical teaching and the location of the tribunal there was surely a reward for such.

Cranmer disputes the heresy charges

A team of scholars was selected to conduct the investigation and the first questions put to them at the tribunal on Saturday 14 April were about the Mass:

- Was the natural body of Christ really in the elements by virtue of the words spoken by the priest?
- Did any other substance remain after the words of consecration?
- Was there a propitiatory sacrifice in the Mass for the sins of the quick and the dead?

In his replies Cranmer skilfully managed to show the confusion among his enquirers about what their theological terms might mean, and he was asked to put his opinions in writing for consideration on the Monday. Over the following days the arguments dragged on. Cranmer acquitted himself well. Dr Hugh Weston, the head of the enquiry team, commented: 'Your wonderful gentle behaviour and modesty, good Mr Dr Cranmer, is worthy much commendation.' But on the Friday, Weston announced (unsurprisingly) that Cranmer had failed to convince with his explanation of the nature of the Eucharist.

The three men were separated, Cranmer returning to Bocardo with more restrictions being imposed on him than previously had been the case. The enquiry had supposedly been established to enquire after the truth of the matters disputed but it was, of course, nothing of the sort. The new regime, aware that the proceedings of the tribunal would not stand up to academic scrutiny, did not publish any official account, nor did it plan any similar events for

subsequent martyrs to present their case before their final
end.

On Saturday 21 April, Dr Weston headed up a triumphant
ceremonial procession through the town holding up the
bread and wine of the sacrament under a canopy of banners
for all to see and worship. Cranmer was forced to watch
from his Oxford prison. But it was seventeen months before
Cranmer was proceeded against, probably because Mary
herself wanted to observe due process, to see Cranmer
officially removed from office, and a new regime put into
place. During this time Cranmer's contact with the outside
world appears to have been limited. It is unlikely that he
knew that Reformers in prison and refugees abroad held him
in high regard and still looked to him for guidance on points
of doctrine and conduct. To know that the Archbishop of
Canterbury did or did not approve of something carried
considerable weight among evangelicals of the day.

Cranmer tried for heresy

Cranmer's formal trial began in the University Church
in Oxford on 12 September 1555. But it was not just his
doctrine on trial, it was his whole career: his marriage, his
public writings, and all his acts as an archbishop in rebellion
to Rome. Cranmer knew that he now faced a more difficult
task compared to that of defending his understanding of the
Eucharist — a long career as archbishop under the control
of the fickle and demanding Henry VIII had produced many
anomalies in his perceived position. Cranmer straightaway
sought to make a distinction between the obedience he
owed to the Crown and his rejection of the pope: 'If I have

transgressed the laws of the land, their Majesties have sufficient authority and power, both from God, and by the ordinance of the realm, to punish me.'

John Story, speaking for the prosecution, suggested that there had been a Catholic Church before there was ever a Christian king in England — the logic here being that Henry had usurped the authority of the long-established church. Cranmer's response to this displays how completely he believed in the church's subordination to Christian princes. He claimed that the early Christian church was defective since 'they were constrained of necessity to take such curates and priests as either they knew themselves to meet thereunto, or else as were commended unto them by other that were so replete with the Spirit of God'. In other words, the leadership and discipline of the early church was defective because it was not led by a monarch. Cranmer, like other Reformers, had no concept of a divide between Church and state. Story countered that the early church was perfect and led by Peter — the only true authority after Christ's ascension.

It is not difficult to see the weakness here of Cranmer's argument, and another prosecutor, Thomas Martin, stepped in, pressing him to answer whether all oaths good or bad have to be obeyed, and then continued by pointing out his changing position on his eucharistic beliefs. Martin did not let up. He asked: 'Who was supreme head of the church?' Cranmer replied: 'Christ.' When Martin asked: 'Not Henry VIII?' Cranmer replied: 'I mean … every king in his home realm and dominion is supreme head.' Martin: 'Was it ever so in Christ's church?' Cranmer: 'It was so.' With a few more thrusts of the argument Martin had Cranmer saying that Nero was indeed head of the church in his own day. Cranmer had not acquitted himself well here as this does not actually seem to have been his position on the matter. Although believing that every Christian owed obedience to their monarch, elsewhere he had said it was only a Christian prince who was head of the church in their own realm.

Cranmer had further difficulty defending his marital status when appointed Archbishop of Canterbury with the church's position on clerical celibacy. In Cranmer's defence, at that time he had declared his intention to 'prosecute and reform matters wheresoever they seem to me to be for the reform of the English Church', and in other disputations at the trial, it is reported that Cranmer did well. Another prosecutor, James Brooks, was particularly stung when Cranmer pointed out that he himself had sworn an oath against the pope in his university career. In his own defence Brooks said, 'I knew not then what an oath did mean, and yet to say the truth, I did it compulsed, compulsed I say by you, master Cranmer; and here were you the author and cause of my perjury.' As MacCulloch comments, virtually every clergyman, civil lawyer, and scholar present that day could say the same.

Cranmer found guilty of heresy

Cranmer was found guilty and in the period after the trial wrote a lengthy defence of his position to Queen Mary re-hearsing again his argument that he was only being loyal to the monarch of the time and pointing out that the Church of Rome had held eucharistic beliefs like his own for many years, transubstantiation being a late invention. On 16 October Ridley and Latimer went defiant to their deaths in front of Balliol College. Cranmer was made to watch the awful spectacle and was apparently traumatized. But it seems that the new Roman Catholic establishment still wanted a recantation from Cranmer, and Cardinal Pole wrote to him suggesting that he could save himself by so doing. A sister of Cranmer (thought to be called Alice), a devout Roman Catholic, appealed directly to the queen for him. It is not clear whether or not this led to the authorities' radical change of policy, but shortly after this, Cranmer was transferred from Bocardo to the deanery at Christchurch. It was a very much more relaxed regime, Cranmer was treated well in pleasant academic surroundings, and he agreed to receive Villagarcia, an able Dominican friar, to dispute with him.

The discussions moved to papal authority and Cranmer reaffirmed a position he had held for some time, namely that a General Council was the ultimate decision-making body for the Church of Rome, not the pope; any such General Council of course meeting only, as Cranmer would see it, with the consent of all the relevant Christian princes of the appointed representatives. He went on to say that if it could be shown that the pope had indeed called all the General Councils (he was convinced that the Council of Nicaea of 325 had not been so) he would happily submit to papal authority. But Villagarcia found documentary evidence suggesting that it was accepted at the time that Pope Sylvester I had called the council held at Nicaea. Cranmer had difficulty refuting that position from the material available at the university, and it seems from this point on that doubts began to arise in his mind. If he was wrong about this, what else had he got wrong?

On 4 December Cranmer was officially deprived of the archbishopric and the necessary steps were set in motion to make Cardinal Pole the new Archbishop of Canterbury.

7

A HEROIC DEATH

England and Cranmer capitulate to Rome

In July 1554, Queen Mary married Prince Philip of Spain. By February of the following year Cardinal Pole had been received into the kingdom as legate of the pope and the Houses of Parliament knelt to receive from him Rome's absolution.

Cuthbert Tunstall, Bishop of Durham, a man for whom Cranmer had always had a high regard, had written a book on the Eucharist that took the same position as the conservative Bishop Gardiner. Cranmer acquired a copy, and it appears he thought Tunstall's arguments carried some weight. Cranmer had now been in prison or under house arrest for nearly two and half years. He had always relied on a small intimate circle of friends and for much of this time they had been denied him; his physical and psychological health were in decline. But it seems he had developed a close relationship with his attendant, Nicholas Woodson, a devout Catholic, and Cranmer began to unburden himself to him.

After holding out so long Cranmer succumbed and went to Mass, but still he refused to accept papal supremacy and this led to an argument with Woodson. It was this breach in a close personal friendship that seemed to have been the last straw for Cranmer — he fainted, collapsing to the floor. He soon after signed his first recantation:

> *Forasmuch as the King and Queen's Majesties, by consent of their Parliament, have received the Pope's authority within his realm, I am content to submit myself to their laws herein, and take the Pope for chief head of this Church of England, so far as God's laws, and the laws and customs of this realm will permit.*

It is telling that Cranmer capitulated, not after a disputation with a mighty theological scholar, nor after watching the horrific burning of Latimer and Ridley in their heroic stand for the gospel, but rather when he thought he had lost the friendship of a person of relatively low social standing. In the subsequent days, Cranmer swung erratically from one position to another, withdrawing previous statements, and then issuing further recantations. Some thought that he might be discharged in light of these recantations but on 14 February the authorities transferred him back to Bocardo prison. This was also the day set for the formal 'disgrading' of Cranmer from the office of Archbishop of Canterbury — a ceremonial defrocking designed to humiliate the victim. He was taken to the church of Christ Church College in Oxford, dressed up in mock versions of his robes, and stripped of them. Throughout the ceremony Cranmer was defiant, and it was then that he appealed his case to a full General Council of the church. He gave six reasons for his appeal, the first three concerned what he saw as procedural violations against him, but the last three defended his previous position against papal authority and the Mass. He was taken back to Bocardo prison from which he did not leave until the day of his death.

Having not expected the appeal, nor the defiance Cranmer displayed during the degrading ceremony, the establishment stepped up the pressure again, and once more Cranmer began to give ground. Villagarcia sarcastically enquired if all the previous saints were now lost because they had not embraced Cranmer's 'new' eucharistic theology. Cranmer said, 'Indeed I think you can attain salvation through your faith and likewise I can in mine.' So Cranmer was saying that to embrace any particular view about the Eucharist is not an essential element of saving faith, a remarkable about-turn by Cranmer that seems to catapult him forwards to the mindset of a future century. The Reformation in England and on the Continent had been dominated by heresy trials about the Eucharist which in turn gave rise to the brutal executions endorsed by both the Church of Rome and evangelicals.

Villagarcia saw Cranmer's statement as a heresy in itself and, on 24 February, the writ arrived in Oxford for the burning of the former archbishop and the date was set. Cranmer now was face-to-face with the awful reality of a grim execution. He was going to experience the same terrible fate that he had witnessed when Latimer and Ridley were burned. It is reported that he trembled in every limb. It is at this low point that he gave assurances to Villagarcia that he wanted to return to the Catholic faith. On 26 February, he signed what seems to have been a prepared recantation. Certainly there was no ambiguity in the words this time; it not only reaffirmed all the key points of Roman Catholic doctrine, it also affirmed that Luther and Zwingli's teaching was indeed heresy. Certainly now Cranmer seemed to experience some sort of release and freedom from guilt as he submitted to the Roman Catholic rite of confession. It is thought Cranmer's Roman Catholic sister travelled again to Oxford to be with him and rejoice in his return to the fold. After being isolated for so long, Cranmer felt that he was with friends again.

News of Cranmer's capitulation spread rapidly from Oxford to London, to the queen and the Privy Council. His recantation was rushed into print, only to be speedily withdrawn. One of the reasons given by historians is that there was a public reaction against it. One of the witness signatories was a Spaniard and this had done nothing to assuage anti-Spanish feeling in the city. But another possible reason is that the recantation had been published without royal permission; that by this time the queen and representatives of the Church of Rome had given up on Cranmer and wanted him executed as a heretic without the complication of a full recantation, which meant under canon law that Cranmer's life could be spared. This is plausible, but it was all too late. The news was out and Cranmer had to sign a further recantation for subsequent publication. As if to underline the fervent nature of the times, a spectacular comet appeared over southern England and remained visible for two weeks, Cranmer himself climbing onto the roof of his prison to view it.

On 17 March Dr Henry Cole arrived to give the news to Cranmer of his impending burning. He seemed to take it calmly and asked that his son should be given consideration for an inheritance, but this was given short shrift by Cole. This particularly upset Cranmer. It is said that that night he suffered a terrible dream where he felt he was both spurned by the monarchy and the church; shut off from both this life and the life to come. He saw the apostle Peter waiting at the gate of heaven; waiting, that is, to turn him away.

The next morning, 18 March, Cranmer signed the last and most abject of his recantations. 20 March was to be Cranmer's last day before his death. He prepared the sermon he was to give at the university church immediately before his execution. He was going to recite it from memory, but was told to write it out as the text had to be available for the officials and for printing afterwards.

Cranmer's last day

On the Saturday morning, the last day of his life, he signed fourteen additional copies of his last recantation. But he was interrupted by a messenger from another of his sisters — one who had embraced the new evangelical faith. She had sent a ring and a note. It seems that this was a turning point for Cranmer; on reading the note he looked across to Nicholas Woodson and said that God would finish what he had begun. It was an enigmatic statement that was soon to have a sharp clarity about it.

Cranmer was led to a specially prepared stand in a very full and excited church; assembled there were various dignitaries to hear the last words of the former Primate of all England. Dr Cole had the tricky job of explaining in his sermon why a repentant sinner still had to be burnt at the stake for heresy. One novel argument that Cole advanced was that the Duke of Northumberland, a layman, had had to be executed in retribution for the death of the layman

Thomas More. And now the execution of the cleric John Fisher would have to be atoned for by the death of the cleric Cranmer. This tit-for-tat vengeance had no basis in canon law and, ironically, Cranmer was the only man in public life who had interceded for the lives of More and Fisher.

Cranmer was listening in tears, but it was now his turn. He took out his prepared text and with immense concentration began to speak. In his opening preamble he gave only this indication that something else was to come: 'yet one thing grieveth my conscience more than all the rest, whereof, God willing, I intend to speak more hereafter'. Cranmer proceeded through his prepared text, but at the moment they expected him to repudiate his earlier writings (that is, what he had written in the past against Roman Catholic doctrine), he instead repudiated his recantations, all he had written 'contrary to the truth which I thought in my heart, and written for fear of death ... all such bills and papers which I have written or signed with my hand since my degradation'.

By now Cranmer was shouting to be heard, such was the noisy reaction of his congregation — some shouting out in anger, others cheering. In a surge of courage, a courage that had deserted him over the previous weeks, he boldly spoke out for the gospel. The old cautious Cranmer was gone. He continued: 'and as for the Pope, I refuse him, as Christ's enemy, and Antichrist, with all his false doctrine'. Above the general din of the congregation he continued: 'and as for the sacrament, I believe as I have taught in my book against the Bishop of Winchester'. At that point he was pulled from the platform by the officials and taken through the streets of Oxford towards his place of execution amid scenes of chaos. It is said that Cranmer strode out so quickly that others could scarcely keep up with him. John Foxe reports that a Spanish friar, unable to understand why Cranmer hadn't preached the sermon that he was supposed to, repeated over and over again as they hurried through the rainy streets of Oxford: 'You didn't do it?'

MacCulloch says,

> In the flames, Cranmer achieved a final serenity; and he fulfilled the promise which he had made in his last shouts in the church: 'forasmuch as my hand offended, writing contrary to my heart, my hand shall be first punished therefor.' He stretched it out into the heart of the fire, for all the spectators to see. He repeated while he could 'his unworthy right-hand', 'this hand hath offended', and also while he could, the dying words of the first martyr, Stephen, 'Lord Jesus receive my spirit ... I see the heavens opened, Jesus standing at the right hand of God.'

By all the most sober contemporary accounts, Cranmer's countenance was indeed serene; the immediate effect of the scene on the crowds, on his Catholic persecutors, and as the news quickly spread, on the English nation and wider European Christendom, was sensational.

What was in his sister's note on the very morning of his death? Was this the catalyst that effected this dramatic change on Cranmer? How had this relatively unknown 'ordinary' Christian woman had such a huge impact on the great Cambridge theologian, ambassador, Primate of all England, and mentor to kings? It is impossible not to see that something she had written was taken up by the Holy Spirit to feed Cranmer's soul in his hour of great need. What an encouragement there is here for us all.

8

AN EVANGELICAL FAITH

As we close our account of Cranmer's life it is useful to look at where he had arrived on his journey of faith on some of the key doctrinal issues of his (and our own) day.

Baptism

Cranmer, like most other Reformers, accepted the practice (if not the teaching) of the Church of Rome regarding infant baptism. Cranmer states: 'Therefore God is both the God of our children, and he also has among those elected to his kingdom, those for whom (since it is not for us to distinguish them from the others) we ought no less than the Early Church devoutly to seek and accept in good faith the grace offered in baptism, as for all our children.' MacCulloch offers the following explanation of Cranmer's position: 'Baptism was therefore only a means of regeneration for those who were already elect; yet humanity must preserve a reverent agnosticism about who those might be, and hence all should be baptized.' *The King's Book* of 1553 (thought to be substantially the work of Cranmer) links baptism with circumcision but rejects that any child dying unbaptized would be lost.

Church and state

Like most Reformers Cranmer saw an intrinsic link between Church and state and that the head of state was the de facto head of the Church. Few evangelical Christians today would adopt such a position, and indeed Cranmer himself found it very difficult to defend, as we have seen, at his trial. MacCulloch comments that Cranmer was 'broken by the muddles of his beliefs about church and Commonwealth.'

Divorce

The Roman Catholic Church did not and still does not believe that there are any grounds for divorce. At the beginning of Edward's reign, Cranmer, based on Jesus' teaching in Matthew 5 and 19, took the view that where a marriage partner had committed adultery both partners to the marriage were free to remarry after divorce, as the adultery had effectively terminated the marriage. But in *Reformatio Legum Eccesiasticarum*, the new canon law code issued during Edward's reign, divorce was allowed for adultery, but only the 'innocent' spouse was allowed to remarry. It is known that Cranmer did not agree with everything taught in this publication. It was the eminent Presbyterian theologian John Murray who pointed out in his 1961 book *Divorce* that it is difficult to discover any biblical grounds to conclude that the remarriage of the guilty divorcee is wrong. This appears to be an example of Cranmer moving further away from Roman Catholicism towards what some see as a more scriptural position, only for the Church in its subsequent formularies to pull back. (A similar example can be seen in the 1552 Eucharist service where the reference to a 'priest' was dropped but reinstated in 1662.)

The Eucharist

It is beyond the scope of this little book to discuss eucharistic theology in sixteenth-century Europe; even Cranmer's own views have been the subject of whole books. It is perhaps easiest to consider the different faith positions as being on a spectrum, with at one end the Roman Catholic position that the bread and wine change and actually become the body and blood of Christ, and so when represented in the Mass, they actually confer grace; and at the other end of the spectrum, the belief that the bread and wine are only symbols and have no intrinsic mystical power. The latter position was adopted by Zwingli in Switzerland, who nevertheless believed the Eucharist to be an important part of Christian worship.

If we move through the spectrum away from the Roman Catholic position we first encounter Luther with his consubstantiation view (the substance of the body and blood of Christ are present alongside the bread and wine, the latter remains unchanged), then we move on to Calvin and Cranmer (who each held similar views), and finally to Zwingli. Cranmer's mature position is stated in his *An answer to a crafty and sophistical cavillation devised by Stephen Gardiner*:

And although Christ be not corporeally in the bread and wine, yet Christ used not so many words, in the mystery of his holy supper, without effectual signification. For he is effectually present, and effectually worketh not in the bread and wine, but in the godly receivers of them, to whom each giveth his own flesh spiritually to feed upon, and his own blood to quench their great inward thirst.

So Cranmer is saying that the emblems effectively signify the body and blood, but any change effected by them is a spiritual one in the believer who takes part in the service.

Justification by faith

Cranmer was as clear about this as he was about unconditional election. Good works formed no part in saving a person from the wrath to come. Good works were only an indication of a person's state of grace, and then only if they proceeded from the once-and-for-all gift from God of saving faith as outlined in Ephesians 2:8-9:

For by grace you have been saved through faith. And this is not your own doing; it is the gift of God, not a result of works, so that no one may boast.

From such a faith flowed the desire to do good works, and furthermore, it was a faith not to be confused with mere intellectual assent. All this Cranmer made clear in his detailed annotations to *The Bishops' Book*, which he wrote for the benefit of Henry VIII.

Preaching

In 1534, Cranmer arranged for Hugh Latimer to preach before Henry VIII's court. He instructed Latimer to read to the audience 'some processes of scripture, the gospel, pistill, or any other part of scripture in the bible' and to expound the text 'according to the pure sense and meaning', and he emphasized the importance in all Christian ministers of 'learning, virtuous example of living, and sincere preaching of the word of God'. Cranmer at this early stage of his reforming career was nailing his colours to the mast and encouraging systematic preaching from an open Bible, and that such preachers should be able students of Scripture and live a life that matched their profession. This was certainly a radical concept in Cranmer's day and even for some churches today.

A priesthood of all believers

The apostle Peter declares: 'you yourselves like living stones are being built up as a spiritual house, to be a holy priesthood, to offer spiritual sacrifices acceptable to God through Jesus Christ' (1 Peter 2:5). From the 1530s it appears that Cranmer had accepted the idea of the priesthood of all believers. He quotes Bede and comments that it is not only bishops and clerics that should be called priests. In 1545, a statute was passed in Parliament allowing laymen to exercise jurisdiction in the church.

Repentance

Cranmer rejected the Roman doctrine of penance and saw repentance as 'a pure conversion of a sinner in heart and mind from his sins unto God'. In other words, repentance was something that happened between the sinner and his God. He saw this as coming from a tender conscience, such a conscience originating in the gift from God of saving faith.

Scripture

From his early academic career Cranmer held a high view of Scripture. It was from this perspective that he assessed the new learning coming from the Continent. Unlike Henry VIII or Thomas Cromwell, he was never interested in acquiring status or political or economic gain from the radical new teaching sweeping through Europe. The evolution of his personal faith, his reform agenda for the Church, and his rewriting of the liturgy were always Scripture-based.

Unconditional election

Although the doctrine is often associated with John Calvin there is no evidence that Cranmer was influenced in any way by the continental Reformer in this matter. Cranmer saw that God controls the world through his sovereign will, and he chooses (elects) from mankind individuals to include in his eternal Church. Cranmer found affirmation for this doctrine in Scripture and in the early Church Fathers (namely Augustine of Hippo 354–430), and it was in turn clearly articulated in Cranmer's *42 Articles of Faith*. This has come to us as Article 17 of the *Thirty-Nine Articles* which were formally adopted by the Church of England in 1563:

> *He hath constantly decreed by his counsel secret to us, so to deliver from curse and damnation those whom he hath chosen in Christ out of mankind, and to bring them by Christ to everlasting salvation.*

Once Cranmer had fully grasped the doctrine of unconditional election, the Roman sacramental system could serve little purpose. And once the *raison d'être* of the sacramental system was undermined, it logically followed that the rest of the Roman Church's edifice fell to the ground. Cranmer (in common with other Reformers) saw this clearly, even if he was not always able to see through to the end the logic of his own position, either in his personal faith or in the reform of the church. Unsurprisingly, after more than a thousand years of the old church's dominance, in both spheres (personal faith and public worship) aspects of Rome's doctrine clung on.

Worship

While rejecting much of the pomp and ceremony of the worship and the liturgy of the Church of Rome, the watchword for Cranmer in this area was caution. As Gerald Bray comments when considering the Cranmer reforms:

> *Theologians may deplore this, but the fact is that alteration in worship style is far more likely to split the congregation*

than heresy preached in the pulpit, which only a minority
can understand. But move the pulpit, turn the communion
table around, or dress the clergy in unfamiliar robes and
everyone knows that something must be going on.

Hooper and Laski both wanted to see more radical reform in worship procedures — a church based more on the Reformed civic churches of Switzerland. Cranmer, while sympathetic to many of their ideals, wanted to proceed by a series of steps taken with the authority of king and parliament while also retaining popular consent; everything was to be done 'decently and in order' as the apostle Paul has said (1 Corinthians 14:40). These considerations often overruled theological purity. It must also be borne in mind that Cranmer had to work in the realm of the possible, he was not able to enforce his own will; for much of his life he had to take into consideration the widely differing views held within the Church as well as the fact that a powerful king with a close interest in these matters was nearly always looking over his shoulder.

In summary

Notwithstanding Cranmer's views on Church and state and his belief in the draconian punishment of heretics, by the end of his life he had arrived at evangelical convictions which meant that he would not be out of place in a twenty-first-century evangelical church. It had been a remarkable journey for a man born in the fifteenth century and consecrated as a medieval Roman Catholic priest.

9

AN ASSESSMENT

Few martyrdoms have had such dramatic or lasting impact on our modern world. The Church of Rome had hoped to triumphantly publicize Cranmer's recantations throughout the Roman Catholic world. Instead the news of Cranmer's courageous defence of the evangelical faith spread rapidly, and within a fortnight, it was the talk of Protestant Europe. Many in England believed that the archbishop's glorious last stand was symbolized by the comet that had been streaking through the sky. Mary's attempts to drag the national church back to Rome suffered a major publicity blow right at the beginning of her short reign.

Cranmer's challenge to the medieval concept of inclusion

As was mentioned in chapter 1, any assessment of a life must consider the times in which it was lived, yet it is difficult for us to fully understand the issues that people felt strongly about nearly five hundred years ago. For example, Roman

Catholicism embraced the whole community. As long as you were baptized as a child (as virtually all were) and submitted to the rest of the sacramental system, you journeyed safely to heaven alongside the rest of the community; none were excluded unless they had excluded themselves by heresy.

In contrast, the new learning was seen to cut like a giant axe through society. The clear Bible teaching that you are justified by faith, and as Ephesians says, 'this is not your own doing; it is the gift of God', separated those that believed from those that didn't believe. Jesus spoke of that intrinsic division in society; it was a division between the lost and the saved. He said, 'Enter by the narrow gate. For the gate is wide and the way is easy that leads to destruction, and those who enter by it are many. For the gate is narrow and the way is hard that leads to life, and those who find it are few' (Matthew 7:13-14). Those faithful to the Church of Rome and its sacramental stepladder to heaven saw that the new evangelical emphasis on personal faith not only undermined the church's teaching, but it also undermined the cohesion of society.

His challenge to the medieval concept of continuity

Furthermore the evangelical 'axe' cut the link between the living and the dead. In the Middle Ages, life and death were thought of as a continuum of existence. People were far more conscious of those that had gone before; week by week in church the names of the recent dead were read out, and on the parish prayer list (bede-roll — i.e. prayer-roll) all the dead from time immemorial were recorded. At the burial service the priest would actually address the corpse

— the dead were living souls continuing their journey just as much as the living were on their own journey on earth. This concept lay behind the fervent devotion to the Mass. When the emblems signifying Christ were presented to God as a sacrifice on the altar during the Mass, the passage of loved ones through purgatory would be eased, but Cranmer's 1552 burial service removed any notion that a liturgical act could do anything further for the dead. The traditional burial rites were about continuity, in the reformed liturgy it became about discontinuity — a separating of the living from the dead. In these bold moves, Cranmer was endeavouring to counter the concept of an ongoing purgatory where saints might intercede for you. Instead, he was reinforcing the biblical teaching that now is the day of salvation, that after death we face the judgement (2 Corinthians 6:2; Hebrews 9:27).

His challenge to the medieval concept of papal authority

Cranmer tackled head-on the authority of the more than one-thousand-year-old office of the pope. Fundamental to the teaching of the Mass was the clerical authority to give the words of consecration. When the priest said these words, he in effect called Jesus down into the bread and wine, and so the Lord of Glory was actually sacrificed again. Cranmer rejected any notion of clerical authority to perform this act, which in turn meant rejecting the source of that authority — the pope. Furthermore, for Cranmer only an earthly king (and certainly not the pope) had the right to appoint senior clerics in the church in his own realm. As has been seen, he extended this concept back through church history and so logically, but to many an evangelical mind today, somewhat bizarrely, he saw the early church in New Testament times as defective without such headship.

His fear of radicalism

The reforms Cranmer was trying to push through the national church were not an obscure argument among scholars about church liturgy, they dramatically impacted people's lives: emotions ran high throughout the nation — from the ploughman in the field to the king himself. Any new movement seeking to be recognized has a natural fear of radicalism. In our own day, many are concerned that the popular revolts springing up in the Islamic world could easily be hijacked by extremists. Cranmer had similar fears and reacted fiercely against those he saw as derailing his attempt to reform the church in an orderly manner, whether they were evangelicals or conservatives.

His ethics

When appointed archbishop in 1533 Cranmer had only just married. Although he might not have been breaking an oath of celibacy, he certainly knew Henry would not be happy with that situation, and so chose to keep the fact secret. It might be thought he could have declined the appointment and simply continued his married life in peace. But this is to misread the situation. The more likely scenario is that Henry would have told him to leave his wife in Germany and take up the appointment. Many might consider Cranmer should have taken this risk and been more open with Henry about his marital position — it is difficult not to see that this would have been the more honourable position. But these were dangerous and turbulent times and Cranmer was rightly apprehensive about how Henry might react.

And why did Cranmer hang on to the office of archbishop in the face of so many difficulties and set-backs in the reform agenda? However, many might see that Cranmer was vindicated, in that by continuing in office, he managed to oversee so many changes that aligned the Church of England liturgy more with evangelical teaching.

But what of the burnings? Even those that might be described as evangelicals were not spared if they did not happen to subscribe to the current orthodoxy. Cranmer's actions here contradicted both natural justice and the teaching of Jesus himself, who clearly repudiated such violence in his name. John Foxe, a contemporary of Cranmer's and author of the well-known book on martyrs, disagreed with any burnings, as did others. And certainly we would all like to think that we would have been one of the few like Foxe who saw the unbiblical nature of these barbarous acts, and had the courage to give voice to that. But can we be sure?

A scholar and family man

There were those, especially early in his archbishopric, who joked about Cranmer's lack of learning. The story is told of one Yorkshire priest regaling his fellows at the local alehouse that the Primate had as much learning as 'the goslings of the green that go yonder'. He was committed to prison by the

Privy Council and languished there several weeks. When Cranmer learned of this, he suggested that the priest might examine Cranmer on a subject of his own choosing. When the priest declined, Cranmer said he would then examine the priest on the Bible (all priests at this time were supposed to be familiar with the Scriptures). Cranmer asked: 'Who was David's father?' When the priest could not answer Cranmer then ventured: 'Who was Solomon's father?' — which again left the priest without an answer. This vignette demonstrates the extent of the problem Cranmer's reforms faced.

In contrast, Arthur James Mason, a biographer of Cranmer, claims that he was one of the most learned men of his age. Writing in 1694 John Strype describes Cranmer's library:

> His library was the Storehouse of Ecclesiastical Writers of all Ages. And which was open for the use of Learned Men. Here old Latimer spent many an hour ... And when Ascham of Cambridg wanted Gregory Nyssen in Greek ... and which it seems the University could not afford, he earnestly entreated Poynet his Grace's Chaplain, to borrow it in his Name, and for his use, for some Months of the Arch-bishop.

John Foxe says that 'this worthy man' would be in his study at five in the morning, and there he would study and pray until nine. He would work during the day on his duties as archbishop but would then often resort to his extensive library and work late into the night to answer questions that Henry would pose to him. A Hebrew Bible that has survived from Cranmer's collection is interleaved with a Latin translation in Cranmer's own hand. It is known that he was also familiar with Greek. Morice says of his home life,

> *Concerning his behaviour towards his family, I think there was never such a master amongst men, both feared and entirely beloved; for as he was a man of most gentle nature, void of all crabbed and churlish conditions, so he could abide no such qualities in any of his servants. But if any such outrageousness were in any of his men or family, the correction of those enormities he always left to the ordering of his officers, who weekly kept a counting-house.*

An unworldly man

Although Cranmer at home enjoyed a comfortable living as archbishop, when Cromwell and many others made themselves fabulously rich at the expense of the disbanded monasteries, he benefited little from the spoils.

He maintained lifelong friendships with many, and it seems that he always looked to see the best in people — certainly an admirable quality, but perhaps his judgement was not always the best. Mason says, 'It is curious how implicitly Cranmer believed that Cromwell — as he had believed that Anne Boleyn — was heart and soul labouring for the promotion of Cranmer's own Gospel.' He pleaded for Cromwell's life as he had pleaded for Anne Boleyn. Although only God knows the heart of the man, it is difficult not to see that Cromwell was using the Reformed cause merely as a vehicle for his own aggrandisement — a fact a more worldly-wise archbishop might well have realized.

A friend of kings

Henry VIII, that most mercurial king, who it is believed executed thousands in his reign, including some of his closest
advisers and of course two of his wives, held Cranmer in
great affection and seemed to take delight in watching and
defeating the plots that were laid against him. Cromwell said
to Cranmer after the archbishop had boldly argued against
the *Six Articles*:

> You were born in a happy hour, I suppose; for do or say
> what you will, the King will always well take it at your
> hand. I must needs confess, that in some things I have
> complained of you unto his Majesty, but all in vain, for he
> will never give credit against you, whatsoever is laid to your
> charge.

A liturgist

One legacy of Cranmer's is that his prose served as the
language of the national church for some four hundred
years. It is a legacy that is not confined to the church, as
MacCulloch says, 'Millions who have never heard of
Cranmer or of the muddled heroism of his death have echoes
of his words in their minds.' At the beginning of the printing
era, when our language was not standardized, it is difficult
to overestimate the role that the *Prayer Book* (alongside the
King James Bible) played in making the English language
what it is today.

Final thoughts

If there is a common thread in Cranmer's life that can be drawn from all the twists and turns of a difficult career, from his mistakes and indecision, from his many doctrinal compromises during the seesaw years of Henry's reign, it is that from 1533 onwards he desired to see the national church reformed along evangelical lines to more faithfully communicate the gospel. It was a consistent driving force. Any Christian today in a responsible position has to decide if and when any particular issue is a resigning matter. Who can judge whether Cranmer had this right or wrong? Certainly if he had resigned at the first hurdle, the cause of the Reformation in England would have been slowed, if not come to a complete halt.

Some might believe that the national Church of England, the result of all of Cranmer's efforts, has confused people as to the nature of true biblical Christianity. But Cranmer's personal journey from the teachings of the Church of Rome to a fully mature 'Scripture only' position and his associated reform agenda was an unfinished one. Had he and Edward VI survived their three score years and ten, it is difficult not to see that the Church of England would have fully embraced the evangelical faith. But Mary's short reign meant that the church was pulled back towards Roman Catholicism, and her successor, Anne Boleyn's daughter, Elizabeth, was keen to end the religious squabbles.

As MacCulloch comments:

Elizabeth ... established a version of the Edwardian church which proved to be a snapshot, frozen in time, of the Church

as it had been in September 1552, ignoring the progress
made in further changing the Church of England after that
date.

Hopefully, we can all learn something from Cranmer's
gentle pragmatism coupled with his determination to hold
to the essentials of the faith. And we can be encouraged that
even though Cranmer had a dreadful time of doubt and
uncertainty in his last months and must have felt that he had
deserted his Saviour, in the end he realized that his Saviour
had not deserted him.

Cranmer's ashes were left in a ditch outside the walls of
Oxford while Bishop Stephen Gardiner, Cranmer's urbane
and worldly-wise opponent (who, unknown to Cranmer, had
died the previous November), was laid to rest in Winchester
Cathedral with all the associated pomp and ceremony. In
the immediate aftermath the conservative establishment
sought to denigrate Cranmer's memory; perhaps in a
sense his reputation has never recovered from this. But it
is difficult not to see that Cranmer, despite his faults, lived
true to his own understanding of Scripture during a difficult
time. Furthermore, his heart, mind and life were directed
towards the furtherance of the gospel. May we be able to
claim as much for ourselves.

RECOMMENDED FURTHER READING

Thomas Cranmer

Ayris, Paul and David Selwyn, eds *Thomas Cranmer: Churchman and Scholar*, Woodbridge, England: The Boydell Press, 1993.

MacCulloch, Diarmaid. *Thomas Cranmer*, New Haven, Conn.: Yale University Press, 1996.

Ridley, Jasper. *Thomas Cranmer*, London: Oxford University Press, 1962.

Background reading

Elton, Geoffrey. *England under the Tudors*, London: Methuen & Co, 1955. Repr., London: Routledge, 1991.

Haigh, Christopher. *English Reformations: Religion, Politics, and Society under the Tudors*, Oxford: Oxford University Press, 1993.

Hamer, Colin. *Anne Boleyn: One short life that changed the English-speaking world*, Leominster, England: Day One, 2007.

Zahl, Paul F. M. *Five Women of the English Reformation*, Grand Rapids: Eerdmans, 2005.

GLOSSARY

Anabaptists
They believed in believers' baptism and the separation of the Church and state. But many had more radical views and some rejected the deity of Christ. They were persecuted by most Reformers.

Annulment
Because divorce was not allowed by the Church of Rome, when a divorce was wanted, a marriage would be declared null.

Communion
See The Eucharist.

Communion in two kinds
This means to receive the bread and wine in the Eucharist service. In the Middle Ages, the practice developed of giving the laity the bread and not the cup to drink — Communion in (or after) one kind.

Convocation

This is a representative body of clergy forming a sort of parliament of the church. Henry VIII's Act of Submission meant that Convocation could only meet with the king's permission and without such no new canons, constitutions or ordinances could be made.

Election

The Reformers saw that the Bible clearly teaches that God had chosen a people to form the church before time began. An example is Ephesians 1:11: 'In him we have obtained an inheritance, having been predestined according to the purpose of him who works all things according to the counsel of his will.' If a person responds to the gospel message and comes to faith they do so because they are one of those so chosen, hence John 10:27-28: 'My sheep hear my voice, and I know them, and they follow me.'

Furthermore God's choice (election), it was believed, was not based on any good works that the person so chosen might do in his or her own lifetime. Hence the doctrine was termed unconditional election. Although associated with John Calvin, it was a key doctrine of the Reformation.

The Eucharist

This is the service instituted by Christ (for example, Matthew 26:26-29), whereby the bread and wine eaten signify in some way the body and blood of Christ. Although evangelicals tend to prefer the term the Lord's Table (or Communion), I have used the term Eucharist as this is perhaps the more usual Anglican terminology.

Evangelical
In the sixteenth century, to be an 'evangelical' meant that you were sympathetic to the new learning that embraced a Scripture-based faith, and that you were less sympathetic to the traditional teaching of the Church of Rome. The use of the term evangelical in the sixteenth century does not imply a full grasp of evangelical principles that might be articulated in the twenty-first century.

The gospel
A shorthand term for the doctrine that an individual is justified by faith in Christ alone and not by any good works, such faith not being from yourself, but rather it is the gift of God.

Holy Roman Emperor
A monarch elected to be the secular ruler of a group of European nations. Charles V (Catherine of Aragon's nephew) held the title from 1519 until 1558.

The Lord's Table
See The Eucharist.

The Mass
A Eucharist service. By the time of the Reformation, the Roman Church taught that in the service the bread and wine actually became the body and blood of Christ. Thus the Mass became a re-enactment of Calvary and could actually 'confer grace' on the recipients and potentially shorten the time in purgatory of a deceased loved one. See The Seven Sacraments.

New learning
A description of the new evangelical teaching emanating primarily from the Continent.

The papacy
This is the office of the pope — the leader of the Church of Rome. At the time of the Reformation, some people were sympathetic to Roman Catholic doctrine and practice but resented the power of the papacy.

A priest
A priest in the Old Testament presented sacrifices to God on behalf of Israel, and so was in effect a mediator between man and God. 1 Timothy 2:5 says, 'For there is one God, and there is one mediator between God and men, the man Christ Jesus.' Evangelicals on the whole see no basis for the priestly office in the church today. Rather, they believe that all believers are in effect priests, as Peter teaches in his first letter (2:5; 2:9).

The Privy Council
This was a body of senior people who would advise the monarch on matters of state. During the reign of Henry VIII the Privy Council, acting with the king, was able to proclaim new laws without calling Parliament.

Purgatory
The Roman Catholic Church teaches that this is a period after death when the soul is purged of any remaining sin.

Saints
The Roman Church defines these as virtuous Christians who have lived in the past and who have been canonized by the church. In the Roman system a believer can pray to

a saint and ask them to intercede for themselves or others here on earth.

The Seven Sacraments[1]

1. Baptism
People baptized according to the rites of the church are freed from sin and reborn as sons of God.

2. Confirmation
Strengthens the supernatural life received at baptism.

3. Eucharist
Known also as the Mass or the Lord's Supper. When the bread and wine is taken, Christ is represented to the Father. 'The Eucharist is not merely an image or symbol of Christ's sacrifice; it is Christ's sacrifice. The sacrifice of Christ and the sacrifice of the Eucharist are one single sacrifice'. The bread and the wine truly become the body and blood of Christ, hence the Eucharist is to be worshipped. Pope John Paul II proclaimed: 'The Church and the world have a great need for Eucharistic worship'.

4. Penance
Supplicants confess their sins to priests who 'by virtue of the sacrament of Holy Orders, have the power to forgive all sins'. When sins are confessed to a priest 'the baptized can be reconciled with God and with the Church'.

5. Marriage
The sacrament of marriage causes baptized Catholics to receive 'actual grace'. The marriage bond is considered to be established by God himself and so is an indissoluble union.

6. Holy orders

'Confers a gift of the Holy Spirit that permits the exercise of a "sacred power" ... After ordination, a priest has the power to turn bread and wine into the Body and Blood of Christ'. 'Priests have received from God a power that he has given neither to angels nor to archangels'.

7. Anointing of the sick

Also known as the last rites, in the sixteenth century it was called 'Extreme Unction' and was primarily performed when the recipient was close to death as a preparation for it. If the person 'has committed sins, he will be forgiven'.

Shrines

The Church of Rome defines a shrine as a church or another sacred place which, by reason of special devotion, is frequented by the faithful as pilgrims. They would often contain a relic, which is an object believed to have come from or to be associated with some holy person.

Vicegerent

A deputy to a head of state — Henry appointed Thomas Cromwell to this position in 1535.

Note

1. Taken from Peter Kreeft's *Catholic Christianity*. This is an official publication of the Roman Catholic Church containing the *Nihil obstat* and *Imprimatur* verifications. Catholic doctrine has changed little over the years, although the church has repudiated the abuses of the system seen in the late Middle Ages. Kreeft, Peter J. *Catholic Christianity: A Complete Catechism of Catholic Beliefs Based on the Catechism of the Catholic Church*. San Francisco: Ignatius Press, 2001.

A wide range of Christian books is available from EP Books. If you would like a free catalogue please write to us or contact us by e-mail. Alternatively, you can view the whole catalogue online at our web sites:

www.epbooks.org
www.epbooks.us

EP BOOKS
Faverdale North,
Darlington, DL3 0PH, England

e-mail: sales@epbooks.org

133 North Hanover Street
Carlisle, PA 17013, USA

e-mail: usasales@epbooks.org